Night of the Grizzlies

NIGHT OF THE GRIZZLIES

JACK OLSEN

HOMESTEAD PUBLISHING
Moose, Wyoming
& San Francisco, California

Library of Congress Cataloging-in-Publication Data
Olsen, Jack.
    Night of the grizzlies / by Jack Olsen.
        p.   cm.
    Originally published : New York : Putnam, 1969.
    ISBN 0-943972-48-5 (alk. paper)
    1. Grizzly bear. 2. Bear attacks. I. Title.
QL737.C2704 1996
599.74'446—dc20   96-3072
                                                      CIP

ISBN 978-0-94397248-0
Printed in China
on recycled, acid free paper.
This edition, 2009.

Photographs by G. George Ostrom, pages 107-109 & 112-118.

9 11 13 15 17 19 20 18 16 14 12 10 8

Published by
HOMESTEAD PUBLISHING
Box 193, Moose, Wyoming 83012
& San Francisco, California 94114

For a complete list of our publications, please check us out at:
homesteadpublishingnet

For Andre Laguerre,
his memory.

ALSO BY JACK OLSEN:

CONTENTS

FOREWORD

On assignment from *Sports Illustrated*, I went to Glacier National Park in 1968 to find out why grizzlies killed twice on one night after decades of non-murderous cohabitation with homo sapiens.

The answer was simple, of course: too many humans infringing on bear habitat, and poor management practices by the National Park Service.

To its credit, the NPS cleaned up its act soon after *Sports Illustrated* ran the three-part series, which was the basis for this book. But that hasn't kept grizzlies from killing again, and again. I hope this work explains why.

Jack Olsen
Spring 1996

NIGHT OF THE GRIZZLIES

Prologue

At first sight, the mountains that fringe the one million acres of Glacier National Park seem bulky, low in profile and broad of shoulder, lacking the sharp needles and spires that the Europeans call *dents* and *aiguilles,* and feel compelled to climb. On some of these lower mountains and hills along the edges of the great park, stark rows of blackened tamaracks reach above the green treeline of the uppermost ridges. Remnants of forest fires of decades ago, they stand on their dead roots in the highest winds and refuse to fall, and somehow they resemble the charred and shattered rows of barbed-wire pickets that remained on the bloodied ridges of World War I. Forest fires, like wars, leave behind the artifacts of futility and uselessness.

Scattered about on the heavily wooded slopes of these foothills of Glacier Park, one sees denuded areas scalloped out of the thick forest as though a giant with a huge bulldozer had come through on an insane joyride. These places are called burns; they mark the more recent fires, the ones that went out of control and laid waste hundreds of acres before enough park rangers and Indians and smoke jumpers and plain citizens could be recruited to return the woods to man's tentative control. In this altitude and this latitude, life returns slowly to the burns, and the colors of the new growth contrast sharply with the deep green of the old, established forest all around. One sees bright yellow bushes a few feet high, multicolored flowers on stalks that reach one's knee, lichens and mosses of orange and purple and umber, and stunted specimens of Engelmann spruce and white pine and larch trying to reestablish a place in the family tree.

The process is slow, the growing season short, the natural obstacles formidable. A beautiful stand of red cedar or giant tamarack may have taken hundreds of years to form, and a sprout that is trampled by an unthinking hiker might not push back through the rocky soil for years. A visitor wobbles off the path and tromps upon the first green shoots of a ponderosa pine seedling and says guiltily to a ranger, "Oh, that's OK, it'll come up again," and the ranger says coldly, "Yes, in ten or twenty years."

Almost invariably, the newcomer to Glacier National Park is overwhelmed first by flora, the tens of thousands of growing plants that are just as much a *raison d'etre* for the park as the grizzly bears and wolverines and marmots that also reside in its interior. Long before one sees the first Columbia ground squirrel or Selkirk marten, one inhales the heady fumes of balsam and picks a path through thick stands of lodgepole pines whose thousands of years of droppings have produced a humus that pushes back against the foot. One pulls up short at broad avenues of wind-felled Douglas firs lying one atop the other like crooked scaffoldings ten or fifteen feet thick, as squirrels and chipmunks scamper in and out of the impenetrable jumble with total disregard for the laws of gravity.

Glacier Park, tucked into the northwest center of Montana,

includes a pair of parallel Rocky Mountain ranges, the Lewis and the Livingstone, and the park's 1,600 square miles spill over on both sides of the Continental Divide. Thus it stands as a sort of windbreak between east and west, catching seeds and spores from all over and turning itself into a display ecosystem of divergent species. Living among the native flora of the northern Rockies are species that blew in from California and Oregon and Washington, from northern Alaska, from Kentucky and Nebraska and New Mexico. In the middle of summer, the park lays down a blanket of wild flowers as variegated as it is short-lived. There are flowers that medicate, like wild sarsaparilla and common self-heal; flowers that can save a man from starvation, like glacier lily and bull thistle; flowers that poison, like American false hellebore and mountain death camas; flowers that induce temporary insanity, like locoweed; flowers that eat meat, like butterwort; flowers that grow on melting ice fields, like white globeflower and Western pasqueflower; flowers that commemorate famous men, like scouler Saint John's wort, and Renaissance flowers of many talents, like Lyall nettle, which stings, offers nourishment, and can be made into fine linen. In the middle of the summer, tall stalks of bear grass adorn the mountainsides like hundreds of twirlers' batons standing upright in the fields, and deep in the cool woods, long black strands of a parasite called squaw-hair lichen or grizzly hair hang down from trees and slide chillingly across one's face like the dangling strings in the fun house. Giant mushrooms pop out overnight in the damp humus; ferns grow man-high along the edges of bogs and streams; berry bushes offer the mixed blessings of sharp thorns and succulent fruit at every turn in the trail.

Naturalist John Muir called Glacier Park "the greatest care-killing scenery" on the North American continent. One's eye is taken not only by the flora but by the geology of this most spectacular of America's wildlife preserves. Millions of years ago, a powerful upthrust from beneath the sea shoved the sedimentary raw material of the park above the waterline of a prehistoric ocean, and glaciers and storms and winds began to carve this huge exposed mass as a small boy carves a block of soap. The result, tens of millions of years later, is a layered jumble of peaks rising to 10,000 feet and bearing on its slopes the clef sign of a time when the only life on the face of the Earth was of the single-cell variety. Here are the oldest sedimentary rocks known to man; they stretch up and up in bands of bright colors, clearly differentiated from the buff-colored weathered limestone near the bottom, through the rich greens of the mudstone argillites and the reds and purples of the Grinnell argillite bands and the high brown limestones called the Siyeh formation. Dotted throughout the various layers, one comes upon reminders that each of these bands of rock was formed under the sea. Stippled rocks show where ancient rains fell on sand that later hardened into the same shape. Thousands of feet up mountainsides, ripple patterns mark the edges of prehistoric beaches, and long, jagged cracks show where mudflats hardened in the sun. On the very tops of peaks, one finds the fossils of fish and shells and plants that once lived beneath the shallow sea that stretched across the North American continent.

In the deep interior of the park, much of the land is above timberline. There are jagged and severe mountains, as broken in their contours as the outlying mountains are smooth, and high on their slopes hang the fifty or sixty glaciers that give the place its name. In winter, the glaciers are almost indistinguishable from the mountainsides; everything is cloaked in a blinding carapace of snow and ice, and edges blur. But as spring arrives and high winds scour the old season's snow off the mountains, the glaciers begin to stand out, pristine and ivory white, and with the coming of summer they remain as visible souvenirs of winter's power and might. As summer wears on, the glaciers shed their outer coats of new whiteness and show the undergarments of rock and dirt and sediment that they have scoured off the face of the mountains with ice pressures in the thousands of tons. Sometimes smaller glaciers disappear entirely, but the larger ones, like Grinnell and Sperry and Harrison, remain as they have for hundreds of years, shrinking and expanding in response to the seasons.

Because of its position astride the Continental Divide, Glacier Park has become part of several watersheds. All winter long, the snows pile up in 20- and 30-foot drifts, and the mountains act as sponges, soaking up the water as it melts drop by drop, then redistributing it, sometimes slowly, sometimes at dangerous speeds, down the mountainsides in the spring and summer. Some of the water winds through the Columbia River drainage to the Pacific; some of it goes east and south to the Atlantic and the Gulf of Mexico, and some of it ebbs northward, to Hudson Bay. From a single 8,000-foot mountain, Triple Divide Peak, the spring thaw cascades into all three watersheds. Everywhere one looks are lakes, some 200 of them, and waterfalls, thousands of them. Here and there, a face of porous rock leaks water through the summer; the most famous of these is called the Weeping Wall, and it stops weeping only in the most arid of years.

The running waters of the park range from tiny trickles oozing out of mountainsides to the larger creeks and rivers, bearing such names as McDonald, Camas, Canyon, Valentine, Red Eagle, Virginia, and St. Mary. All of the streams drain lake systems, and all are full of the colorful cutthroat trout, so named for the orange-red slashes across their throats. In some of the creeks, Dolly Varden trout up to 20 pounds battle their way to the ends of the tiniest tributaries to spawn. This most predatory of the American trout is called locally by the ignominious name "bull trout," in a familiarity bred of proximity. The bull trout lives to spawn again, but its distant relative, the kokanee salmon, gives up the ghost in the reproduction process and thereby provides the wherewithal for one of nature's most lavish affairs. The "kokes" leave Lake

McDonald each September to spawn and die in the waters of McDonald Creek just inside the southern border of Glacier Park, and hardly has the run begun before every fish eater for miles around is racing toward the scene. The bald eagle, symbol of America's might and freedom, flies in and takes up its perch on a tree alongside the water's edge, its telescopic eyes scanning the pools and riffles for dead salmon. In one year, 352 bald eagles were counted in a stretch of the creek measuring little more than a mile. Also in attendance each fall are golden eagles and snowy owls, sports-loving species that prefer to catch their kokanee alive. In the social structure of this particular outdoor banquet, the snowy owl, an annual visitor from the Arctic, is dominant. Sometimes bald eagles are shooed away from fish by the large white owls, and although the national bird is better equipped for combat, it does not seem to know this and invariably retreats. Later, perhaps to revitalize its sense of self-worth, the eagle may bully an osprey, swooping down to make the industrious fish hawk drop its dinner in mid-flight. The bald eagle also retreats, but with far better reason, from the black bears and occasional grizzlies that come to the dinner, but it does not seem especially frightened of another guest at the affair, the coyote, who arrives as a sort of cleanup detail and crunches away until the very last bone of the very last salmon has been converted into fuel for another long winter.

Because they are completely protected from hunters, Glacier Park's wild animals, such as the coyote, are slightly more tolerant of man than are animals outside the park, although there is not a wild coyote alive that will allow *Homo sapiens* such liberties as getting close and trying to make friends. But if the visitor is selfish and patient and utilizes such aids as binoculars and spotting scopes, Glacier Park's animals will surrender their secrets easily. Halfway up Camas Creek, the hiker comes to a broad, swampy meadow, and far across on the other side, perhaps a quarter of a mile away, two clumps of brown fur stand motionless. Slowly, *slowly,* the hiker raises binoculars and brings into sharp focus a large animal standing alongside a perfect miniature of itself. The downcurving Roman nose and the clump of fur dangling from the chin identify the large animal as a Shiras moose, and the miniature quickly identifies itself as a close relative: It butts its mouth sharply against the underside of the mother for a sip of milk, leans away to munch on a mouthful of tender willow shoots, then reaches under the mother's soft belly for another taste of milk. The mother looks over her shoulder, and the hiker could swear she gives the weaning calf a dirty look; the time has come for the young animal to enter moosehood, to stop living in two worlds, and the hiker senses that any day now the mother will make her feeding equipment unavailable to the splayfooted calf at her side.

Farther up the stream is a pool created by those industrious dam builders, the beavers, survivors of the beaver-coat fad of the '20s and '30s and the merciless trapping techniques of early woodsmen. Beavers are to be found in substantial numbers all over the Rockies, particularly in the haven called Glacier Park, but now one sees nothing in the pool except a narrow wake that leads out of sight behind some fresh-cut logs. Then one hears the crack, as loud as a pistol shot and just as unnerving. The beaver has whacked the surface of the water with his broad tail and thus warned other beavers in the neighborhood that a large non-beaver is on the premises. Now the animal is safely inside his lodge, his place of concealment given away by the tiny puffs of breath-fog that come out of the topside vent in the chilly morning air of the high mountains.

Swinging through Glacier Park on nature walks, one never knows where to look; there is so much animal life around that the unexpected soon fades into the ordinary. One walks softly alongside a narrow stream, hoping to come upon an otter slide or see the flash of silver that marks a fleeing trout, but instead one rounds a narrow curve and blinks one's eyes in disbelief:

A mouse is chasing a water bug *across the surface* of a pool. All day long, one wonders, but later the nature guide ends the confusion. The mouse was not a mouse at all, but a water shrew, *Sorex palustris navigator,* a tiny hunter with a pointed nose and webbed feet and blinding speed that enable it to romp across pools without breaking through the surface tension. The same nature guide reveals that the *Cinereus* shrew, a cousin of the water shrew, is the smallest mammal found in the park, almost never reaching four inches in length and seldom seen by humans. Its life expectancy is almost as short as its body; hawks, owls, and some of the carnivorous mammals wage a constant war on these diminutive animals, often killing one and contemptuously leaving the little carcass behind as not worth the bother.

Wending one's way farther up the stream, and perhaps daydreaming a bit as the warming sun begins to climb above the treetops, one suddenly becomes aware of a loud hissing sound. In a few more steps, the source of all this anachronistic theatrical noise is found huddled in a narrow cut just below the lip of the bank. The rich brown fur, the tiny patches of white on the chin and throat, and the elongated weasel-like body identify the animal as a mink, one of the bravest and surliest beasts, pound for pound, on the face of the Earth. The larger meat eaters of the park have long since learned that a mink is trouble, and only a few species, such as the horned owl, are considered natural enemies of the feisty aquatic animal with the expensive coat. The mink does not seek out man, but neither does he back away, and long after one continues along the stream, the hissing continues; one wishes that the little beast would shut up lest all the wildlife for miles around be scared away. But there is no danger of that: The fauna of Glacier Park is so rich and varied that it is all but impossible to walk more than a mile without seeing something, perhaps merely a snowshoe rabbit or a Columbia ground squirrel or a Rocky Mountain jumping mouse, but *something.*

Often the seeker after wildlife is stunned by the sight of specimens that would be considered minor miracles of observation
if they were spotted outside the limits of the park. There are
places near Sperry Glacier where it is a rare day when mountain goats are *not* visible. Around Many Glacier, a small herd
of Rocky Mountain bighorn sheep usually is grazing, and a
short hike to a nearby overlook will reward the student with
a closer view of these prized and rare animals. Elk may be
seen along the middle branch of the Flathead River in such
numbers that the Park Service has had to consider ways and
means of thinning out the herd; there are some 3,000 of the
big deerlike mammals in the park, and they are overgrazing
their winter range.

Although Glacier Park no longer is home to certain extinct
or nearly extinct animals like the bison and the kit fox, it is the
last hiding place for several other endangered or rare species.
The Rocky Mountain wolf, a noble animal that may weigh as
much as 200 pounds and sport a coat of purest white, has all
but disappeared from its vast North American habitat, and up
to a few years ago, it was thought to be absent from Glacier
Park as well. But lately the animal has returned, in small but
definite numbers. Many of the "wolf" sightings in the park
turn out to be large coyotes, but there have been enough
sightings by experts to guarantee that the Rocky Mountain
wolf remains in the Rocky Mountains, at least in that portion
called Glacier Park.

Although the glamorous animal known to mammalogists as
Felis concolor missoulensis has all but disappeared from the area
around Glacier Park, some are seen each year within the park
boundaries, where they apparently have sensed that they cannot be hunted. *Felis concolor* is the mountain lion, alias cougar,
painter, catamount, panther, and puma, and there is no place in
the world where this shy, secretive animal may be considered
common. Even in Glacier Park, one will almost never see a
mountain lion, but sometimes one will spot the track of the

cat in fresh snow. It is big and round and unmistakable, and the sight of it gives one a momentary fright, even though the catamount's personal habits make it about as dangerous to man as the water shrew chasing a bug across a mountain pool.

The wolverine, perhaps even more rare than the mountain lion, carries its heavy weight of legend about Glacier Park and sometimes is seen high-tailing it toward the nearest patch of deep woods. It is said that the wolverine can follow a trapline and remove all the kills and bait without getting caught, that it sometimes will attack and kill moose and elk, and that it will stand up to any animal in the forest, including the bear and the mountain lion. In point of fact, none of these claims can be documented; there are so few wolverines to be observed that folklore has moved in to take the place of science. One can be certain only that the wolverine packs 25 to 35 pounds on a rugged, ursiform body, that it is a close relative of the skunk, and that it prefers to mind its own business. Like most members of the weasel family, the wolverine is a powerful hunter, but it certainly is not the moose killer of Western legend.

The largest of all carnivores in the continental United States, indeed a subspecies of the largest of the world's terrestrial carnivores, also is to be found within the confines of Glacier Park, although it is doubtful that the species will survive many more decades of nearness to man. The observer may prowl the backcountry of the park for weeks without spotting a specimen of *Ursus arctos horribilis,* but then suddenly a broad expanse of silver and brown will stir into motion in the bushes ahead, rise to its full height of seven or eight feet, shake its great shaggy head from side to side, and disappear into the forest at a speed that belies its quarter ton of sinew and fur and muscle. Then the observer will find that his heart is pounding with mingled fear and pride, and he will rush back to the lodge or the camp or the cabin to tell everyone that he has seen with his own eyes, in its own natural setting and on its own terms, the grandest animal of the North American continent, an animal whose qualities of courage, independence, and intelligence overshadow the bald eagle as a symbol of America.

The bear is called grizzly because his silvery white-tipped fur looked, to the early explorers who named him, like the gray in an old man's hair. Webster still defines "grizzled" as "sprinkled or streaked with gray," although the word seldom is used nowadays. The grizzly is grizzled, to be sure, but there are wide variations from bear to bear and observer to observer. A grizzly standing in dark shadow in the deep woods may show no silver whatever; seconds later, backlighted by the clear blue sky, he may look as though he has been frosted in a subzero blizzard.

Grizzlies also vary in their underlying color, and the big bear comes in every conceivable shade of black, brown, and white and all possible combinations, from pure white through cream, buff, burnt umber, sienna, chocolate, charcoal gray, charcoal black, midnight black, and gradations in between. To make matters of identification more confusing, some grizzlies have fur of two or even three different shades, or swatches down the back or across the shoulders, or varying colors on their faces and ears and jowls, and all grizzlies change color slightly through the year. Thus it comes as no surprise to naturalists when six people look at the same grizzly and offer six different descriptions.

All will agree, however, that *Ursus arctos horribilis* is large, powerfully built, extremely wide across the head, and possessed of a hump above the shoulders that makes him unmistakably a grizzly and not a black bear, *Ursus americana,* the only other bear species common to the continental United States. As the grizzly moves along a trail, its heavy head swings from side to side, the better to sniff the wind and examine the surroundings through its extremely poor eyes. With its hump and its short back legs, the grizzly looks like an animal trudging uphill. But if something should arouse it, such as the most insignificant whiff of man smell, the illusion of ponderousness is immediately dispelled, and the grizzly is sprinting away and out of sight with a speed that eternally confuses those who think of all large bears as slow and ungainly. The grizzly's speed is somewhere between the speeds of man and horse. Based on estimates made by those few who have been able to clock the animal over measured distances, the big bear would beat the world's fastest humans by 30 or 35 yards in the 100-yard dash, and by a third to a half mile in the mile run. In forest terms, this means that a grizzly on a ridge 300 yards away can be at one's side in twenty seconds if he chooses to be. Fortunately, not one grizzly in 10,000 chooses to be.

Anatomically, the grizzly is a magnificently designed machine with heavy, powerful muscles, thick bones of dense cellular structure, and a collection of joints that are loose and flexible, similar in principle to the universal joints of an automobile, enabling the animal to function from almost any position. The teeth are canine and the molars large, equipping the grizzly for both cutting and grinding, and the jaws are powered by two massive muscles that make the side of the bear's head seem to jut out and enable him to crunch through almost anything softer than steel. The muscles of his forelegs are similarly oversized, and there are numerous cases on record of grizzlies fracturing the skulls of bull elk and full-grown horses with a single swipe. As if the front paws were not lethal enough already, they are equipped with curving claws from four to six inches long, useful for the digging that grizzlies enjoy and the fighting that they usually try to avoid. All four feet are plantigrade, like man's, with rudimentary heels and balls and nails in the form of the razor-sharp claws.

The grizzly's hearing is about equal to man's, his eyes markedly inferior, his nose one of the sharpest in the animal kingdom. Woodsmen used to say, "The pine needle fell. The eagle saw it. The deer heard it. The bear smelled it." Indeed, if the grizzly does not smell something, he remains doubtful that it is there, even if the something is as big as a house. Because he stands alone at the top of the North American peck order, the grizzly is not in the least reluctant to approach anything that moves until he gets close enough to make a positive identification, either with his inferior eyes or his superior nose. Sometimes this approach is made at top speed, and many a hiker in places like Glacier Park has had the wits scared out of him by a grizzly that seemed to be charging down the wind at him but at the last second whirled about and ran upwind twice as fast. Some park officials attribute at least half of all reported grizzly "attacks" to the phenomenon of the bear's poor eyesight and limitless curiosity, which sometimes cause him to get closer than he himself intends to get. In almost every case, the grizzly will depart at high speed the instant he recognizes his one natural enemy on Earth: man. This does not keep the unsuspecting human from climbing trees first and asking questions afterward. Not frequently, but often enough to keep the hiker honest, a grizzly will keep right on going and bowl his victim over. This is part of the animal's vast reservoir of unpredictability, an unpredictability that is the quintessential nature of the beast. Former *Sports Illustrated* editor-conservationist André Laguerre had a saying to the effect that no statement about wildlife is more than 60 percent true; in the case of the grizzly bear, one is tempted to lop off an additional 10 or 20 percent. For example, it has been recorded for decades that grizzlies cannot climb trees, this inability having something to do with the tremendous weight they must pull up with muscles made for other uses. But every four or five years, someone reports a case of a grizzly high in a tree, chasing another animal or looking for some greenery to stuff in his stomach. One such report of a tree-climbing grizzly came from Jasper, Alberta, Canada, and the observer may be reckoned to have known what he was talking about: The bear, enraged about something or other, was coming up the tree after *him*. It reached him, pulled him down, and knocked him silly.

If there is such a thing as a creature of habit *and* unpredictability, it is *Ursus horribilis*. In some of the wilder parts of their habitat, grizzlies frequent trails used by other bears, and the result is a peculiar sort of path with a high crown a few inches wide in the middle and two deep ruts alongside, where the heavy claws of hundreds of bears have scraped away the dirt. There are grizzly paths where individual steps have been worn into the ground by habit-bound bears literally following in the footsteps of others. Another bear habit is the scratching of long slashes in trees, and one can tell when a grizzly is around by the exceptional height of the marking.

Female grizzlies keep their cubs with them for two years or more, and during that time they evidence no interest in matters of sex. When at last the female is ready to accept a mate and begin another family, she puts the male grizzly through an absolute hell of frenzied anticipation. For days, she will allow him to follow her around, but she will not permit him to lay a paw on her in passion. The two bears will play together, sleep alongside each other, hunt as a pair, and stuff their stomachs together, but until the female is good and ready, they will not unite in physical matrimony. Each time the randy male comes too close, the sow lopes away, and the fatigued suitor must follow her and await his chance or go and seek another mate who will only treat him the same. When the great event takes place, after days and days of frustration and miles and miles of travel, it lasts for twenty or thirty minutes, and then the two big furry lovers scurry toward different points of the compass as though they can no longer stand the sight of each other.

The cubs are born in hibernation in the dead of winter and, at birth, are blind, helpless and small. But after a few months of constant suckling of the mother, the young bears come out of hibernation weighing as much as 25 pounds, glossy of coat and ready for instant mischief. Up to a point, the mother grizzly will play happily with her cubs, sometimes for hours at a time. She will cuff them about gently, sitting on her rump and beckoning them to come on in and mix it up, and she will suffer their scratchings and clawings almost to the point of drawn blood before calling off the fun. Hikers have seen mother bears and their cubs lying in seep pools and swamps against the summer heat or splashing one another with water in a brook. Others have seen bear families enjoying snowslides and snow fights just before hibernating together for another year. The mother grizzly seems possessed of an almost infinite amount of patience and love for her cubs, and she will fight to the death for them. It is only when the young bears are willfully disobedient, especially in the training courses given by the mother on such important subjects as berry hunting, squirrel digging, and man avoiding, that she will insist on absolute obedience, reaching out to smack a feckless cub with the same paw that can brain a Percheron.

Except for their offspring, the grizzlies of North America appear to live for their stomachs. Wrote Canadian Andy Russell, in his fascinating book *Grizzly Country* (New York, Alfred A. Knopf, Inc. 1967):

> The grizzly joins man, the hog, and the common rat in being the four outstanding omnivores on Earth. Like them, he will eat almost anything when hungry and a great variety of things most of the time. It would be much easier to list the things the grizzly does not eat than those he does.... Most of the time the grizzly follows his nose through life; wandering from one smell to another, always seeking, nearly always hungry, but as carefree and happy as an animal can get. He makes use of his natural endowments to the fullest, fitting his way to conditions as they are found. Probably a grizzly bear's idea of pure heaven is a mountain slope glistening with the blue-black shine of huckleberries hanging thickly on the bushes, the brilliant glow of buffalo berries, or the luscious smell of acres of wild raspberries, strawberries, and saskatoons.

For the grizzly, life is a glorious saga of nip and crunch and lick and swallow, and it matters little what is being nipped and crunched and licked and swallowed. The same grizzly that will devour 40 pounds of maggoty venison that has been lying in the sun for a week will stop by the nearest anthill for a nightcap on his way home, probably for the tangy taste of the formic acid that abounds in the ants' bodies. Grizzlies will watch pine squirrels bury hundreds of nuts from white pine cones, then spend days digging up the industrious workers' winter storage. There is no other way for the bears to get the tasty nuts; they grow at the very tops of the trees, far past the reach even of the lighter black bears, and if it were not for the squirrels, the grizzlies would never know this delicacy.

The long, sharp claws on a grizzly's forefeet are perfectly suited to the job of digging, and except for the berries that he strips from bushes and crams into his mouth at a breakneck pace, the big animal gets most of his food by using his paws as pick and shovel. When glacier lilies begin to appear, grizzlies cannot be far behind. As the flowers burst into bloom higher and higher on the mountainsides, the animals follow the harvest like *braceros*. In their compulsion to get the succulent glacier lily bulbs, sometimes they manage to convert solid swatches of real estate into disaster areas. When they come to a patch of grass, they will graze on it like cattle, and when they come to the burrow of a Columbia ground squirrel or a gopher, they will flail away at the earth with such unabashed enterprise that they will sometimes dig themselves almost out of sight, expending far more energy than ever could be regained from the insignificant food value in the victim. Grizzlies are disproportionately fond of marmot, the so-called whistle pig that weighs up to a dozen pounds and builds its home in cracks in solid rock or under stones so huge that not even the most powerful grizzly could budge them. Nevertheless, grizzlies persist in trying to eat up every marmot in sight, sometimes spending hours on their labors and enlarging great cavities in the side of the mountain, while the marmots sit securely inside their impenetrable strongholds, whistling merrily and picking their teeth. A visitor to Glacier Park swears that he watched through binoculars as a grizzly dug for a marmot for two hours. Every now and then, the bear would stop to inspect the point of attack and scratch his ear, for all the world like a puzzled demolition engineer working out a special problem. At the end of the time, a new cave had been added to the rocky talus, and a very weary bear was trudging away, looking back over his shoulder in some sort of ursine embarrassment, perhaps to see if any other animal were watching. Grizzlies do things like that. Outdoorsmen have told of stumbling on grizzlies in the deep woods, to the great surprise of both man and beast, and watching as the frightened animals ran several hundred yards before turning around and beginning a charge right back toward the scene of the encounter. Twenty or thirty yards away, they will pull up in a cloud of dust and then march imperiously away. "There is only one conclusion I can draw from that," said the victim of one such strange encounter, "and that is that the grizzly has pride. He wanted to run away ... and *stay away,* but first he wanted me to know that he wasn't afraid to come charging back. He was *embarrassed* at the way he ran the first time!"

Years ago, there were few such anthropocentric attempts to understand the mighty bear that stalked the Western plains by the hundreds of thousands. The early settlers were oriented toward hunger and pain and vicissitude, but most of all they were oriented toward menace, and the first interpretation of the huge bears with the long, canine teeth and the massive curving claws was that they were a threat to life. When it was discovered that each such "threat" also produced several hundred pounds of edible meat, the grizzly's fate was sealed. The subsequent history of the great bear can be told in a word: attrition. Grizzlies were shot, strangled, poisoned, trapped, and generally harassed all across the old range that extended west from the Mississippi River and south into Mexico and north as far as Alaska. In the High Sierras of California, home of a tawny subspecies called *Ursus magister,* farmers and ranchers distributed poison with utter disregard for all forms of animal life and killed off the last golden bear in 1922. The state that had presided over the annihilation of this grizzly subspecies selected an official state animal: *Ursus magister.* The University of California still calls its athletic teams the Golden Bears; they are the only such bears in the world.

One by one, the conservationists of other Western states reported the extirpation of the grizzly within their state borders, and when the West was finally and irrevocably won and hundreds of thousands of Americans rolled across the United States to take up their homes and homesteads in the grizzly's old domain, the big bear was visited with the ultimate punishment: the destruction of the forests in which he could hide, the plowing of the plains on which he grazed, the stringing of thousands of miles of barbed wire, and the pervading, unpleasant stink of man, who only smells good to himself and his fellow man, and not always then. The grizzly of the plains, as was his custom, backed into the final square miles of American wilderness, avoiding a fight. He is holed up there today, his numbers reduced to less than 1,000, perhaps as few as 500, his range restricted more or less to a few states: Montana, Wyoming, Idaho, with eight or ten individuals in the Cascade Mountains of Washington and perhaps two or three more in Colorado. (There are some 25,000 to 35,000 grizzlies of varying subspecies in Canada and Alaska, but they may be considered permanent exiles or foreigners; those grizzlies that fled northward from the continental United States will never return, and the native grizzlies of Canada and Alaska are slowly disappearing as the bulldozer and the road grader continue their implacable march northward.)

The tragic flight of the grizzly, the species' gallant battle merely to remain alive as an American species, has not gone unnoticed, and a mystique has grown stronger since *Ursus horribilis* has been placed on the endangered list and the future is uncertain. There is a protectivism about the grizzly, and humans—who might have gleefully hunted the noble animal some 75 years ago—now go about bemoaning the fact that certain states still permit his slaughter. There has developed a mixed sense of admiration and solicitude and pride about the grizzly; he is seen as the prime example of America's maverick own, something that did not come over in a ship, something unmistakably native to the land.

A psychologist might say that some of this protective attitude toward the grizzly is related to the country's guilt about the cruel treatment of the species, but a simpler explanation is the traditional Yankee veneration of the courageous underdog. "Dogs, guns, poison and traps have swept the majority of grizzlies away," Enos Mills wrote in *The Grizzly*. "Their retreat was masterly and heroic, but the odds were overwhelming." Gradually the great bear ceased to be a menace and became a source of pride, and readers could stir to the words of dedicated conservationists like Andy Russell, who bared his own feelings in *Grizzly Country*:

> The animal that impresses me most, the one I find myself liking more and more, is the grizzly. No sight encountered in the wilds is quite so stirring as those massive, clawed tracks pressed into mud or snow. No sight is quite so impressive as that of the great bear stalking across some mountain slope with the fur of his silvery robe rippling over his mighty muscles. His is a dignity and power matched by no other in the North American wilderness. To share a mountain with him for awhile is a privilege and an adventure like no other.

Russell, who may be the ranking nonscientific authority on the grizzly, calls him "the living symbol of the mountain wilderness" and new generations of outdoor Americans, the backpacking fresh-air seekers who are spilling into the national parks in record numbers, are inclined to agree. There is no thrill like returning to St. Louis or Chicago or New York with a tale about a grizzly that came in the night and stole a package of cookies and ran off when someone shouted, "Get out of there, you old son of a gun, you!" The thrill comes from close camaraderie with "the living symbol of the mountain wilderness," the kinship of sharing the forest together, and ultimately the feeling that the huge animal with the consummate tools of murder on his paws and in his mouth chose instead to run away like a shy child.

Out of all these commingled feelings about the great bear, conscious and unconscious feelings, expressed and implied feelings, has come an admiration of the grizzly that borders on hero worship, especially on the parts of those who live near the final haunts of the animals or come into these areas to hike and enjoy nature. When a rogue grizzly must be exterminated by government officials, the laments of these new ursophiles continue for months, and letters to the editor run four or five to one in condemnation of the exterminators. On those rare occasions when a grizzly makes an attack on a human being, or *appears* to make an attack, there is an automatic response by those who control wildlife areas to give the animal another chance, to wait and see. Says Mel Ruder, Pulitzer Prize-winning Montana editor and longtime student of grizzlies and people, "Montana is one of the last remaining places that have grizzlies, and there's a strong sentiment to protect the grizzly. And in the national parks, that feeling is even stronger. 'Grizzlies must be preserved at all costs'—that's what they'll tell you. So when any attacks would happen, the park officials would just let nature take its course, hoping that nothing else would happen."

Ruben Hart, a former chief park ranger at Glacier National Park, was not reluctant to express his feelings about grizzlies. "I've got all the respect in the world for those critters," Hart says. "They've been pushed back by man, pushed back and pushed back, all the way into the mountains. We have to think twice before we kill one, and think twice again."

Park officials like Ruben Hart are the stewards of the grizzlies' last days as an American species, and most observers will agree that they are performing the difficult task as well as can be expected. When Yellowstone Park was created in 1872, grizzlies imploded into the protected area, where probably 200 or fewer of them remain, and when Glacier Park was set up in 1910, the grizzlies seemed to sense once again that this was a place where hunters could not follow, and something between 100 and 140 of the great bears remain within the relatively narrow confines of the park today. The number varies with the month; when the Montana hunting season begins, grizzlies scurry out of the Bob Marshall Wilderness Area and the Flathead National Forest and the Blackfeet Indian Reservation, all contiguous with Glacier Park, into the safety of the area where firearms are not allowed.

The men who preside over America's national parks operate under a clear and simple mandate. The act of August 25, 1916, creating the National Park Service, said that the function of the new government agency would be "to conserve the scenery, the natural and historic objects and the wildlife" and "to provide for the enjoyment of the same in such manner and by such means as will leave them unimpaired for the enjoyment of future generations." Later, the same philosophy was laid down in the Park Service's administrative manual:

> The animals indigenous to the parks shall be protected, restored if practicable, and their welfare in a natural wild state perpetuated.... Their management shall consist only of measures conforming with the basic laws and which are essential to the maintenance of population and their natural environments in a healthy condition.

All the legislation and all the policy statements added up to a paraphrase of Mies van der Rohe's famous approach to the science of design: "Less is more." The national parks were to be administered with the least amount of human interference consistent with keeping wildlife "in a natural wild state" for "the enjoyment of future generations."

For decades, that simple approach worked to perfection. In the case of the grizzlies, more and more of them holed up in the national parks, especially Yellowstone and Glacier, where they presented no problem. In 1911, the first full year of Glacier Park's existence, there were only 4,000 hungry visitors, and very few of them went into the craggy backcountry where grizzlies were enjoying their independence and the freedom from man's meddling that had been denied them for nearly 100 years. Later, guided horse trips into the park's interior became popular, and long packtrains would travel from camp to camp in tours that might last a week and cover hundreds of miles of grizzly habitat. As many as 10,000 horsemen a year were visiting Glacier in the years just preceding World War II, but grizzly incidents were all but unknown. By the time the loud parties of humans and their sweat-lathered horses drew near the den of one of the great bears, the animal would be five miles away with its tail between its legs. In the first 30 years of the park's existence, only one human being was harmed by grizzlies. John Daubney hiked into Piegan Pass in 1939 and was slashed by one of a trio of grizzlies that attacked him. Nevertheless the park's animal safety record was vastly better than any zoo's in the country.

But after World War II, the situation changed. The packhorse concession had folded during the war, and people started going into the park on foot and in great numbers. Hiking has remained popular with the park's visitors. By 1966, nearly a million people a year were coming to Glacier, and some 30,000 of them were hitting the wilderness trails into the backcountry. Footwear had been improved, lightweight clothing had been perfected, plastic tents and aluminum backpacks were available, and dudes who had never spent a night in the open were finding themselves marching deep into the interior of Glacier Park and the very heart of the grizzly refuge. Once again, the bears were confronted with their only natural enemy, and once again they retreated; but the hikers' lemminglike rush continued, and all at once the simple mandate of the National Park Service had become exceedingly difficult to administer. Minor brushes between man and bear became a part of each summer's history, and new rules crept into the Park Service manuals. "Remove by shooting those known and identifiable rogue bears that cannot be transplanted promptly and efficiently by trapping or by drugs," one such rule specified. "Superintendents, at their discretion, can authorize park rangers to destroy an individual bear in any emergency or after a verified report of a personal injury." (Realizing the public sympathy that was building up for the embattled species, the cautious author of this directive added, "When a bear is to be removed by shooting, it should be done discreetly and with as little public attention as possible. We must realize, however, that such a positive approach to the problem will cause some visitor reaction that may or may not be friendly.")

And so the National Park Service, an agency dedicated by law to the preservation, protection, and restoration of the wild-animal species in the park, found itself more and more in the business of trapping and transplanting and sometimes shooting the rare grizzlies to protect tenderfooted hikers. At first, the necessary killings were accomplished almost in secret. Said Dave Thompson, West Glacier businessman and frequent park visitor, "Twenty, twenty-five years ago, somebody would come in and say they were bothered by a grizzly, and automatically some ranger would go out quietly with a gun, and that would be the last you heard of that bear."

No ranger was fond of the job, but it had to be done. Man-grizzly incidents were becoming more common, and ranger executives feared an outbreak of maulings. No longer could Glacier National Park be administered as a giant culture dish in which representative types of American flora and fauna were completely protected to the exclusion of all other considerations. With his probings deeper and deeper into the wilderness retreats of the great bear, man was pressing harder and harder against the patience of the grizzlies, and the animals themselves were finding less and less space in which to flee the dreaded man smell. In August, 1956, a man named Tobey Johnson was bitten by a grizzly while sleeping in the open at Stoney Indian Pass. This was the first attack on a human by a grizzly since the 1939 incident at Piegan Pass, and only the second such attack recorded in the park's previous history. In the next ten years, there were nine more attacks, and three of them resulted in serious injury. The mystery was not that there had been so many attacks, but so few. Tens of thousands of visitors were sifting into the farthest reaches of the park, but despite this intense pressure, the administrators of Glacier Park could report at the beginning of 1967 that in its long history, not a single life had been lost to the world's largest land carnivore. Apparently the Park Service's improvised policy of shooting or transplanting troublesome specimens was working successfully. To be sure, there were a few voices crying out that sooner or later human life would be sacrificed unless fewer hikers were permitted to leave the trailheads or the bear population was drastically reduced or wiped out entirely. One advocate of grizzly extermination, Forest "Nick" Carter, was himself a former chief ranger at Glacier National Park. Carter told the *Hungry Horse News,* a northern Montana weekly newspaper, that "the government has to take the decided step to safeguard the trail traveler from grizzlies and do it before some hiker loses his life."

But no one was listening to Nick Carter, and in fact there were some rangers, just as sincere and dedicated as their former chief, who suggested that he must be getting cranky in his old age. One had only to look at the record. As a ranger executive explained it, "If you set up a danger index ranging from zero to ten, where the butterfly is zero and the rattlesnake is ten, the grizzlies of Glacier Park would have to rate somewhere between zero and one. The rattlesnake kills about ten Americans a year. The grizzly kills about none. It's foolish to talk about the grizzly menace to human life."

Admittedly, there were a few mysterious deaths on the books of Glacier Park, a few people who had left the trails and never been seen again, alive or dead. But the fact remained that as the long, hot summer of 1967 began, park officials could boast with accuracy that not a single documented death could be blamed on the embattled grizzly.

— 1 —

THAT SUMMER: KELLY'S CAMP

A few miles inside the southern edge of Glacier National Park, the visitor comes to Lake McDonald, ten miles long and nearly two miles wide, glowing with the intense blue-green common to deep glacial lakes all over the world. On windy days, the spindrift on the lake catches the sun's rays and sends off glittering arcs of light like shooting stars. When the wind dies, the water turns into a translucent turquoise, weightless and unfathomable, and children dangle their heads over the sides of boats and try to see to China.

Millennia ago, an immense glacier came inching into a vast basin of soft rock and carved out Lake McDonald as one would slice the eye from a potato. For at least three-quarters of its length, the lake is 400 feet deep, with sharp drop-offs on all sides. Lake trout, the atomic submarines of freshwater, cruise about at maximum depth, hunting for baitfish that enjoy the same environment, and above them are several varieties of trout and vast schools of algae-eating whitefish, whose flesh is as tender and mild as turbot or sole. Every now and then, an osprey swoops down to the lake's surface for a snack, and most of the time his victim turns out to be a whitefish. Perhaps the herbivorous little fish is less skilled at evading the fish hawk, or perhaps the osprey is a gourmet with sophisticated tastebuds; there is no definitive answer, and neither osprey nor whitefish is talking.

Ducks and swans and geese live at Lake McDonald, too, and one sees grebes, sandpipers, gulls, terns, and other typical water birds soaring around the lake, seeking their own kinds of provender. Sporadically, one is rewarded with a glimpse of the rare Grinnell water thrush, teetering on the littoral of the lake, using its tail as a balance rod. Deeper in the woods, noisy mountain chickadees, metallic-blue Steller's jays and hen-sized ravens make their homes among the coniferous trees that flourish at the 3,000-foot altitude. Some of them live in stands of Western red cedar, sometimes called arborvitae, or tree of life, by botanists. The red cedar gives off a spicy, pungent aroma and resists decay for ages, long after fire or disease or pestilence has ended its natural life in the forest. Not far from Lake McDonald, one can see the spars of dead red-cedar trees poking like monuments high into the sky. Around the red-cedar populations are patches of Western larch, or tamarack, one of the few cone bearers that shed their needles. In early autumn, the needles of the tamarack begin to fall like maple leaves, leaving its bare trunk and branches reaching into the sky like the fingers of the dead. In spring, new needles appear in a pale-lime color that makes the tree stand out from the other species around it, and soon the thick overhead branches of all the coniferous trees blend together in a mottled green canopy that shuts out the sun and makes the forest below seem coolly primeval.

At the northern end of Lake McDonald, in a fern-filled mossy copse among such trees, a small collection of cabins traces its existence back to the years before Glacier Park was founded. Nowadays, the place called Kelly's Camp is owned by descendants of the original settlers who homesteaded the land and refused to sell it to the government, thereby retaining possession even though completely surrounded by publicly owned land. Kelly's Camp is a serene and silent place, sheltered from the sun by the stately trees and sound-conditioned by the beds of needles that mute the footsteps and the voices of the good neighbors who live there in the summer.

Early in the summer season of 1967, one of the first to arrive was Mrs. Don Berry of Ephrata, Washington, a schoolteacher descended from the original homesteader. Together with her three children, ranging in age from 6 to 16, Joan Berry moved into her customary dwelling: "the big house," largest of the various cabins and dwellings on the property and the one traditionally reserved for descendants of the original Kelly family. Her husband, Don, would commute back and forth to his radio station in Ephrata.

It was shortly after the middle of June when Mrs. Berry first saw the bear. She glanced out the back window of the big house toward a little indented area, where garbage and trash barrels were kept, and saw an animal that puzzled her. Joan Berry was no stranger to grizzlies after a lifetime of summers in Glacier National Park, and this bear was plainly a grizzly, with its dished-in face and conspicuous hump just behind the head. But she had never seen so ragged a bear. One expected grizzlies to be somewhat mangy and dull in the early summer, after a winter of hibernation, but this bear's physical appearance was markedly worse than average. The hair on the mane behind the hump, usually luxuriously thick, was short and thin, and when the animal leaned over to dip into the Berry family's trash barrel, Mrs. Berry could see bald spots along the line of the backbone. The head seemed long and narrow, almost misshapen; to Mrs. Berry, it looked like a normal grizzly's head that had been flattened and stretched. When the bear rose to tip the big fifty-gallon drum just outside the back window, the

schoolteacher got a good look at its claws; they were longer
than any she had ever seen, and it occurred to her that the bear
must not have been using them for normal pursuits like digging
for roots and small mammals and other delicacies; hence they
were not being worn down properly. She supposed that the
grizzly might be an old-timer barely managing to hold onto life
by scrounging for garbage. Certainly the animal was underfed;
it had the frame of a large bear, upwards of 500 pounds, but the
body was so emaciated and scrawny that Mrs. Berry doubted
if it would weigh half that much. She concluded that the grizzly was not only elderly but sick, and she decided to mention
the pathetic old specimen to one of her ranger friends when
they happened along. There was no hurry; grizzly bears were
not uncommon around the thick woods of Kelly's Camp, and
in all the years since the original Kelly had established the
homestead, no one had been killed or injured by them. Usually the bears would run at the first sight or sound of human
beings and confine their petty pilferings to the small hours
of the morning when the camp was silent and asleep. But as
the first weeks of summer passed, Mrs. Berry noticed that the
strange bear was as different from other grizzlies in action as
it was in appearance. She would look up from her housework
in the primitive cabin and see the animal digging into the trash
barrels in broad daylight, and when she would make tentative noises to frighten the bear away, it would stand and look
at her unabashedly or even take a few menacing steps in her
direction. She warned the children about the bear and told
them that it could not be treated as a normal, nervous grizzly
that would run away. When they saw the bear in the corners
of the camp, they were to come indoors immediately.

Soon the bear was visiting the garbage cans behind the
big house every three days, almost like clockwork, and the
scholarly Mrs. Berry had become the resident authority on the
peculiar animal. She watched it engage in quixotic unbearlike
behavior night after night. One evening, the animal suddenly

flew into a rage, dumped all the garbage cans and flung them about like matchboxes, and just as suddenly reared up on its hind legs and began to bat playfully at the moths flitting in the light above. A few minutes later, the grizzly dropped back on all fours and continued tearing up everything in sight.

After only a few visits, the bear seemed to become acutely annoyed by motion inside the house, and it would charge the walls or slap at the tiny window panes with its claws. Whenever the mercurial grizzly was at the garbage cans, Mrs. Berry would counsel everyone not to move between the light and the window, and if someone would forget and commit this error, the bear would crash into the side of the house with all its weight, smashing against the walls with its heavy paws and one night sending a saw flying halfway across the room from the intensity of the impact.

The Berrys had disciplined themselves to remain completely inert when the bear was around, but they could not discipline their German shorthaired pointer. If the dog would bark when the bear was outside, the result would be an instant attack. Whenever someone spotted the bear nearby, Mrs. Berry would grab the dog and hustle him into a room on the opposite side of the house from the garbage cans, where neither animal would sense the other's presence. But sometimes she was too late. One night, as she lay in bed, she heard the familiar noises from the garbage cans. The bear was right on schedule; it had been exactly three days since its last visit. Mrs. Berry jumped out of bed and ran to get the dog, but the big pointer had heard the noises himself and raced into the kitchen, barking and growling. Almost in the same second, there was a thump, and the back door started to buckle inward. Mrs. Berry held her breath as the bear crashed into the door once again, and she pulled and shoved the dog into another room and locked him in. The next time she looked out the back window, the bear was calmly selecting foodstuffs from the cans, as though nothing had happened to disturb its equanimity. Mrs. Berry thought that there must be something wrong with its brain.

A few days after this incident, Kelly's Camp was noisy for a change. The day was bright, and the camp was full of vacationers and multiples of their children, running about between the tall trees and splashing around the lakeside. Up on the porch of cabin No. 2, a feast had been laid out on a big table. There were bologna, cheese, ham and all sorts of delicacies, and liquid refreshments of various proofs down to zero. A good time was going to be had by all, for this June 29, 1967, was the fifty-seventh birthday of one of the most popular of the camp's regular guests: Mr. W. R. "Teet" Hammond, a kind and gentle man who spoke with a soft Lyndon Johnson accent and wore a cowboy hat.

W. R. "Teet" Hammond was the sort of person who is called by his nickname by young and old alike, this despite the fact that he was a man of imposing stature who once had been sheriff of Clayton, New Mexico, a dry and dusty place that was almost the exact reciprocal of Kelly's Camp. With his wife, Hammond had been spending summers at Kelly's Camp since 1955, and he had long since come to be regarded as the unofficial marshal of the place, though he neither liked guns nor understood them to any great extent, despite his past experience. One might have supposed that a man like Hammond, in his twelfth season deep in the interior of Glacier National Park, would know all there was to know about things like grizzly bears. But he did not. "Far as me knowin' anything about grizzlies, other than to chunk 'em and pop 'em if you have to, that's it," he once explained. "Other'n that, I've never been too interested in grizzlies." Personally, he preferred to don his old five-gallon straw hat and row out on the lake for a try at the trout and salmon. Indeed, although it was his birthday and the festivities were about to begin, Teet Hammond was puttering around the lakeside as usual. It was about five in the afternoon, and a new boat had just been delivered, and Teet and a few of his friends were helping to launch it. The boat had barely tipped the edge of the cold water when Teet heard a commotion and turned to find his wife running at top speed and hollering for his attention.

"There's a grizzly in camp!" she cried.

Teet stopped what he was doing and considered the matter. Finally he said, "Ah, blooey! There's no such thing as a grizzly here in the last of June. Early in the spring and late in the summer, yes, but never in the middle of the summer. It's impossible."

That was that. If Teet Hammond said it was impossible, it was impossible. The men turned back to the boat, and Mrs. Hammond watched. But hardly had they returned to their task when somebody said, "Look over there at the impossible!" and Teet looked and saw a big, furry animal at the outer edge of the bay.

"Run get the binoculars and let me get a look at that," Teet said. "Now I'm not so sure *what* it is."

A few minutes later, Hammond was narrowing down the focus of his binoculars, and at last he had a clear and distinct look at the animal. "It's a grizzly, all right," the former sheriff said, "but I never saw one like this before. He's got a pretty good-size frame, but he's poor! He's skinny and thin lookin', like he doesn't eat. He is surely poor! "

As though insulted by the description, the bear turned and dipped into the woods, and when it did not come back into sight, the men finished launching the boat and strolled up to cabin No. 2 for the birthday party. One by one, the other guests arrived, and soon there were nine on the wooden porch. They were singing "Happy Birthday to You" and "He's a Jolly Good Fellow" and other tributes that embarrassed Teet Hammond to no end, and then somebody served a few drinks. The poor grizzly was forgotten, until one of the birthday celebrants strolled to the end of the porch and looked down the steep flight of eight or ten rough-hewn steps that led to the forest floor and saw the bear standing there taking it all in.

Somebody shouted, "Get the food inside!" and Teet rushed to get a close-up look at the grizzly before it could run away. As he watched from the head of the stairs, the bear calmly began walking toward the cabin. Teet shouted at it and made a few threatening gestures, but the grizzly continued on a straight line toward the foot of the steps. When the animal reached the bottom and began climbing, Teet shouted for everybody to get inside and picked up a heavy bench about four feet long. The animal was halfway up the steps when Teet lifted the bench above his head and sent it crashing down. The edge of the bench seemed to hit the bear's foot, but the animal showed neither pain nor panic. It backed down the stairs, stood up on its hind feet and snorted once or twice, then dropped down and walked slowly into the brush.

Once again, the party was resumed, but only a few minutes had passed when Teet heard screams from the south end of the camp. Someone was hollering, "Get a gun! "

Teet went to his cabin and picked up his old lever-action .25-.35 and hurried toward the noises. On the way, he met his 9-year-old grandson and a girl of about 14 walking rapidly along the dirt road. Just as they reached Teet, the boy said in a loud whisper, "Don't run, but walk as fast as you can!" Teet looked down the road and saw the bear coming toward them at a range of about sixty feet. While the children rushed toward a cabin, Teet levered a cartridge into the chamber, clicked off the safety, and drew a bead on the hurrying animal, and when it was clear to him that the grizzly was not going to slow down, he fired a warning shot into the dirt about three feet from the bear. The animal stopped short and then rose to its hind feet in the classic position of attack. Teet cocked the gun again and raised it to his shoulder, and as he did he said to himself, "Well, he's fixin' to come now. I'll just have to get him."

He held the grizzly's head square in his sights, and he was about to begin a slow squeeze on the trigger when the animal dropped down and circled around the back of a cabin. Teet waited, and a short time later he heard a scream from the big house, where the Kelly descendants stayed. He rushed over with his rifle cocked, but the bear had dashed to another part of the camp. Teet ran to his telephone and called park headquarters for help. An hour and four phone calls later, the bear was still foraging around the camp, and no ranger had arrived. It was almost dark when the frightened citizens of Kelly's Camp heard the sound of a vehicle driving up and two armed rangers got out. They explained that they were sorry it had taken them so long to arrive, but they had been attending a first-aid course. They told the people not to worry, that they had seen the bear scurrying up the ridge toward Trout Lake as they had driven toward the camp.

"I don't claim to be an authority on bears," Teet Hammond spoke up, "but I'll tell you one thing for sure. That bear wasn't acting right. No, sir, that was no normal bear."

The rangers said they would check into the matter, but for the time being they felt that there was no danger. After all, the bear was running away when they spotted it. An animal that ran away could not be considered much of a menace to human life. Teet Hammond said he hoped that they were right, but that it had taken the bear an awful long time to make up its mind to run away.

A few days later, a ranger executive arrived in Kelly's Camp on a routine visit, and Joan Berry, who had been away from the camp on the bear's most recent intrusion, took him to one side and said, "We've got a sick bear, a crazy-acting bear around, and I wish you'd do something about it."

The official asked for a description of the animal, and Mrs. Berry told him that it was a dark grizzly with a big, emaciated frame and a thin, elongated head. "I'm sure that he's dangerous and somebody's going to get hurt," the schoolteacher said.

The ranger executive chuckled at the remark. "Oh, Joan," he said casually, "is it really that bad?"

Mrs. Berry was annoyed and repeated emphatically that

the bear was acting abnormally and must be considered a menace.

The ranger official said, "Well, when his illness makes him go berserk, we'll do something about him," and made it plain that the matter was closed. His attitude made Mrs. Berry seethe inside. In all the decades since her family had homesteaded on the north shore of Lake McDonald, they had almost never reported a troublesome bear; they preferred taking their chances on coexistence. Kellys and grizzlies had been living together amicably since the 1800s, and Mrs. Berry felt that the ranger official ought to know that and ought to have taken her complaint more seriously.

∞

The next weeks were spent in a state of tension. The grizzly came back periodically, and the residents of Kelly's Camp drove about with rifles and shotguns on the seats of their cars and kept careful watch on their children and their pets. The Park Service, badgered by dozens of complaining calls from the families of the camp, installed a big, green trap, but the strange grizzly ignored it. Several times, rangers arrived with guns, but they were always a few minutes behind the wary animal. It seemed to have a particular fear of automobile or truck engines, a fear that was not accompanied by a similar response to marine engines. Several times, the bear walked right up toward motorboaters trolling the edge of the lake, but the instant an automobile engine would come into earshot of Kelly's Camp, the grizzly would scamper off.

One morning, in the last cool hour before dawn, an elderly resident of a camp a few miles down the lakeshore heard a noise exactly like a thumbnail screeching across a violin sounding board. Jim Hindle jumped out of his bed and grabbed his gun; he thought he knew exactly what was making the sound— he had been hearing about a peculiar bear for weeks—and he wanted to put an end to it once and for all. Hindle dashed out of the bedroom toward the screeching sound, and sure enough, two panels had been neatly slashed and bits of light screen were flapping in the morning breeze. Hindle could see the bear, a tall, skinny grizzly, standing about ten feet away, but when he poked the barrel of the gun through the hole in the screen, the bear moved behind a butane gas tank and out of the line of fire.

Jim Hindle had been coming to Glacier National Park for nearly four decades, or about four times as long as any of the park rangers, and it infuriated him that this misshapen grizzly with the collection of weird habits was still at large to rip open his screen and endanger both him and his wife. He shoved the slug-loaded, double-barreled shotgun under his arm and pushed open the door to the outside to solve the problem, just as he had solved any number of bear problems around the camp in the past. His right hand was missing, but Jim Hindle was not afraid of mischievous bears, whatever their dimensions.

Outside, it was still half dark, but Hindle could see a portion of the bear as it ran behind a tall fence on the other side of the lawn. For an instant, the bear rose to its full height above the six-foot fence and exposed part of its head and shoulders, but before Hindle could fire a single barrel, the animal was off and running. There was no possibility of taking a shot at the fleeing shadow; the camp was full of people, including many children, and a wounded grizzly was the last thing Jim Hindle wanted. He waited a few minutes for the animal to return, but then he heard a dog barking excitedly a mile or so up the lake, and he knew that the bear was making tracks.

At nine that morning, Jim Hindle knocked loudly on the door of the nearby Lake McDonald ranger station, but the ranger was away. The angry man telephoned his information straight into headquarters, and there was no time lost on cordial conversation. Hindle was a well-known critic of the National Park Service; for forty years he had been telling the park how to get by, and for forty years the park had been ignoring his every suggestion. His latest suggestion was that something had better be done about this crazy grizzly before somebody was killed.

Park officials answered the retired schoolteacher's latest blast by sending a part-time employee, a college student, to conduct an interview. "He wanted to know if I was sure it was a grizzly," Hindle told friends later, "and I said, 'Son, I've seen more grizzlies than you have flies!' Then he wanted to know if I had gotten a look at the bear's teeth and whether there was any tartar on them and what color the eyes were and I said no, I hadn't observed any of those important things. But then I told him that they should destroy that bear, because it was too bold and the fear of man had gone from it. I said if you don't, the federal government is liable to have one of the darndest lawsuits that they ever had if this bear kills. This boy said something to me about preserving the species, and I said, how many sharks do we have to have in the ocean to preserve the shark species? I told him I thought the park spends too much time thinking about the preservation of the species and to hell with the preservation of the people."

The upshot of this confrontation was a crisp report in the park files. "This is probably the same bear which hangs around Kelly's Camp," the report said. "No real damage reported; just rummaging for food...." The report was filed; no action was taken.

Not long afterward, Teet Hammond was being visited by a good friend, Lou Feirstein, a Montana lumberman and rancher, when the telephone rang and one of the Berry children announced that their mother was off shopping and the bear had arrived. What should they do?

"Just wait right there, honey," Teet said. He and Feirstein grabbed up rifles, walked to the big house, and tiptoed through the front door to a rear bedroom that overlooked the trash cans. The bear was only six or eight feet from them, going about its business of pilfering garbage and swatting millers, and all that separated men from grizzly was a window with tiny panes. Wordlessly, Hammond and Feirstein stretched out on the cot in the darkened room and sighted their rifles on the bear's head from a prone position. But no shot rang out; each man was waiting for the other. Teet was troubled by the memory of a woman in the camp who thought the grizzly was cute. One day, when the bear was standing just outside the window, the lady had tapped on the pane and said baby words to the big teddy bear. What would someone like that say if he blasted the animal's brains out? Teet held his fire while he puzzled out the situation. Finally, he said, "You know we're not supposed to shoot him unless he comes in a building or destroys something."

"I'm just a visitor, and I'm not supposed to shoot him at all," Feirstein said, "but I sure would if I owned property here."

The two cronies watched the bear through their sights for ten minutes, then ten minutes more and ten minutes more. Once, the grizzly flew into a rage over nothing and slapped the window in front of their eyes, but the thick glass held, and just as suddenly the bear returned to its battle with the garbage cans, turning them upside down and scattering the smelly refuse all over the ground. When it appeared that all the edibles might be gone and the bear about to go on its way, Hammond said in a soft voice to the visiting rancher, "I'll tell you how we can do it and nobody'll ever know who shot him, Lou. We'll count one-two-three, and we'll both pull the trigger, and we'll blow him in two." But before Lou Feirstein could comment, the grizzly was gone.

When August 1 arrived, the inhabitants of Kelly's Camp recapitulated the bear's pattern: Since the middle of June, it had visited the place some fifteen times, starting at first in a cycle of every three days, extending this to four, and now arriving every fifth day on a rigid schedule. But then a ranger dropped by and told some of the residents, "You shouldn't be having any more trouble. Your bear's at Trout Lake, tearing up camps." For the first time that summer, Kelly's Camp relaxed.

— 2 —

THAT SUMMER: TROUT LAKE

F our miles up and over Howe Ridge, the place called Trout Lake was popular with fishermen because of a peculiar combination of circumstances: It was close enough to an automobile road to be reasonably accessible, but the climb up and down the spiny back of the ridge was steep enough to keep out the dudes who were beginning to clutter up certain other wilderness campsites in the park. To get to Trout Lake from Lake McDonald, hikers had to hit the trail not far from Kelly's Camp and climb 2,000 feet in two miles, a rate that quickly eliminated any but the most serious of hikers. Once on top of the ridge, it was an easy 1,500-foot descent through the forest to the lush stand of vegetation that made the place popular with another sort of wildlife—bears, both grizzly and black. There was hardly a spot in Glacier Park where more grizzly sightings had been made; in fact, a trio of visitors to Trout Lake once reported being treed by no less than five grizzlies simultaneously, something of a record for the National Park Service.

In recent years, the trail register just below the lake had been crammed with entries about bears. If they chose, campers could make comments in the book, placed in a small cabinet alongside the road. Rangers had to laugh when they read one day, "I just came face to face with a grizzly bear," followed by an entry that said, "I saw the pile that the lady left that came face to face with the grizzly bear."

The reason for Trout Lake's surplus of bears was Trout Lake's surplus of berries, the strawberries and raspberries and most of all the huckleberries and serviceberries that constitute the bear family's basic diet. There are other berries that grow in the region of Trout Lake, but they are less tasty, and bears ignore them until they have no choice, like children eating their cauliflower last. Typical of these unloved specimens are the thimbleberries that grow all around the lake; the fruit resembles raspberries and comes in a beautiful dull-red color, but the flavor is flat and insipid and does not live up to its promise. Neither does the bearberry, with its dry and seedy fruit. The Indians found a better use for the bright red bearberry; they ground its leaves, called it *kinninnick,* and smoked it incessantly. Bears eat it, instead, but only as a last resort.

In those rare years when the huckleberry crop comes up short around Trout Lake, the bears have even been known to turn to tart, unpleasant berries like those produced by the twinberry varieties, red and black, and even the Pacific mountain ash, whose red-orange berries form a large, fiery clump that one often sees decorating the front yards of North American towns. But no bear will touch a shrub called smooth Menziesia, or fool's huckleberry, which grows in the region of Trout Lake and confuses the tourists. Through the years, the bears have learned that the blue-black berries of the Menziesia are small, hard, and totally inedible, and the leaves are poisonous if consumed in large quantities. The grizzlies do not consume them in large quantities, or small quantities either, nor are they fooled by two other tempting plants of the region: showy crazyweed (also known as hairy locoweed) and little larkspur, both of which are poisonous.

Almost all of these specimens, the tasty ones and the flat ones and the downright evil ones, are to be found struggling for *Lebensraum* on the mountainsides around Trout Lake. In places, the greenery looks almost tropical, as though patches of Brazilian rain forest had been laid down intact like thick green throw rugs. Old paths wind through the brush, and there are places where one can stand and pick whortleberries from both sides of the trail, if one is so inclined. A thousand bears could hide in this thick growth of bushes and flowers and shrubs and never be seen by man, and many a fisherman has whipped his dry fly on Trout Lake in happy ignorance of the fact that a collection of burping grizzlies was lapping up berries just a few hundred yards away.

The lake itself lies in a bowl rimmed by mountains that tower thousands of feet above and duplicate themselves almost perfectly in the clear blue-green of the water. Camas Creek flows in the north end and out the south, and at the lower outlet of the lake, several hundred huge tamarack trunks are crunched together into a logjam that will support a man's weight almost all the way across the water; the tamaracks have long since lost their bark and their branches to the grinding action of the weather, and now they flash white in the sun like a stack of bleached bones. To one side of the logjam, a small clearing has been hacked out of the spruces and thick bushes that march down to the water's edge; in its center, the Park Service has installed an iron grating for cooking, and the spot is popular with campers, who pitch their tents, drag a few cutthroat trout out of the lake, and enjoy an epicure's feast in the forest.

On the afternoon of June 25, 1967, a week or so after the strangely shaped grizzly had first been spotted at Kelly's Camp, a pair of 22-year-old honeymooners arrived at this campsite. Peter Cummings, a medical student at Western

Reserve University in Cleveland, Ohio, and his law-student bride, Ellen, intended to spend the night in the open and then push on for a three- or four-day hike into the vast interior of the l-million-acre park. Their plans had been made with meticulous care. Before setting foot on the trail, they had checked out the possibility of grizzly attack. They had been told that the only genuine danger might come from stumbling across some cubs and being chased by an overprotective mother who thought she was defending her young. They were advised that the possibility of attack was so remote as to be almost ludicrous, but if they were nervous, they could carry bear bells that jingled on their packs and presumably warned all wild animals that humans were coming. The young honeymooners armed themselves with the bells, and just before pushing out into the wilderness, they talked briefly with a ranger who told them that they had been in far greater danger on their drive from Cleveland than they would be on their hike.

Toward the end of this first day on the trail, Peter and Ellen had begun to accept the idea that the ranger was right. They had reached the logjam without so much as seeing a trace of bears, either grizzly or black, and now they were getting ready to enjoy their dinner. Peter had pitched their tent, and Ellen had dished out heaping hot portions of canned ravioli, and they were about to dig in when a crash came from the fire-grate area, where their provisions and gear were piled temporarily. Unconcerned, Peter Cummings told his wife to look out and see what was there; she was sitting closer to the tent flap. When Ellen refused on the reasonable grounds that she was a woman and strange noises frightened her, Peter pulled the flap aside and saw that a grizzly bear had walked into the middle of their camp and was engaged in popping open tin cans with its teeth. He motioned to his wife to be silent, then gripped her hand and half pulled and half led her out of the tent and up toward the trail. The bear showed no interest in them as they passed eight feet away.

When they had reached a point about 150 feet up the lake, the young couple stopped for breath, and then they saw two people fishing a little farther up the shoreline. The four gathered together on the trail and exchanged ideas. Everyone was nervous, but no one was very frightened. They all had been informed over and over that wild bears in this wild park could be counted upon to run from humans, and they assumed that it was just a matter of minutes before the bear would realize that it was acting in a very bizarre manner and move on. They stood and watched; their view was limited in the gathering dusk, but the bear appeared to be a skinny brownish grizzly with a peculiarly long, thin head. It was busily biting into cans and ripping into the canvas packs. When Peter Cummings saw that their entire supply of food was being ruined by this presumptuous animal, he began to shout, and others joined in the clamor. "Hey, get out!" someone said, and the others cried, "Go home, bear!" "You're not wanted!" The situation was annoying, to be sure, but not without its lighter side.

The animal did not even cock an ear in the direction of the sounds. Slowly, systematically, it went about the business of destroying the camp. When the provisions and gear were littered about, the grizzly turned to the tent and ripped it open with a single claw, as though it were pulling down a zipper. Inside the tent, it continued the job of demolishing the worldly effects of the young couple from Cleveland. Twenty-five minutes after the attack had started, the grizzly casually ambled down to the lakeside, about 30 feet from the wreckage, and began lapping at the cool water. "Come on!" Peter Cummings said to his wife, and the two of them tiptoed back to their camp. While the bear occupied itself a few bounds away from them, they looked for salvage. Of their fifteen or so cans of food, all but two had been opened. Peter's extra set of long underwear had been chewed into strips and now stank of bear. The first-aid kit was ripped open. The aluminum pack frames were bent out of shape. The tent was shredded.

Once again, the young husband put his fingers to his lips to caution his wife against making a sound. They picked up the undamaged sleeping bags and reached for the remains of their packs, and one of their warning bells, tied to a pack, began to tinkle. The bear looked up and headed immediately in their direction. Peter and Ellen held onto what was left of their belongings and raced up the trail to a shelter cabin two miles away near Arrow Lake.

On their way out by daylight, the couple spotted fresh bear scat, but they saw no grizzlies, and after an hour's walk, they reached Trout Lake. There they recognized a short-time acquaintance from the village of West Glacier, a young man who had told them a few days before that his father worked for the Park Service. He was fishing, and he gave the famished couple a trout, which they cooked and ate on the spot. When they told him what had happened, the young man expressed no surprise. "That same bear bothered some people a few weeks ago," he said. "They're gonna tranquilize him and ship him north of here."

At ranger headquarters just outside the village of West Glacier, the couple filled out a report about the ruined gear. A courteous ranger seemed to enjoy talking to them, but he asked one question that was perplexing. "What was the bear's name?" the ranger said.

The couple answered, "Huh?"

"What was the bear's name?" the ranger asked. When Peter and Ellen persisted in looking blankly at him, he explained that sometimes bears get nicknames after they have disturbed a sufficient number of people.

"No," Peter Cummings said finally. "We didn't get his name."

∞

For the next month or so, the bear without a name alternated between harassing the people of Kelly's Camp and making raids on the itinerants who were flowing in and out of

Trout Lake in great numbers. No physical contact was made between man and bear, although there were times when the peculiar animal would follow campers for hundreds of yards, always staying twenty or twenty-five feet away, and scare them half to death. Almost always the victims of such encounters berated themselves later, the tenderfeet for not knowing that grizzlies are relatively harmless, and the old-timers for realizing it and still being afraid. There was something about this persistent grizzly that alarmed even the most knowledgeable. Grizzlies had been snooping in and out of the campsites of North America ever since the first primitive man had pitched the first camp, but they had rarely made their intrusions while the campsites were occupied, and certainly not while people were in the middle of meals and other activities. The oddly shaped grizzly did not seem to know fear, nor did it seem to understand the ground rules that always had been followed by man and bear in Glacier National Park. It stormed into camps and bowled over fire tripods, tents, and packs; it stayed exactly as long as it wanted to stay; it ignored the shouts and screams and sometimes the rocks of annoyed and displaced campers.

The rules of the National Park Service specify clearly that such a bear must be shot, but somehow the skinny animal managed to remain alive through June and July. Now and then, an ashen-faced camper would make a report in person, and others would scribble capsule comments on the trail registers. But no one was reading the trail register (they were to be gathered at the *end* of the season and studied), and no one seemed to be listening to the first-person reports. A biology teacher named Ron Johns and his small children were shadowed by the bear for several hours, and when they made a complaint to rangers, they were told that the animal should have been eliminated but the rangers simply had not had time. Two hikers from California were treed by the bear and their packs rifled. When they reported the incident to a ranger executive, they were told that others had encountered the same grizzly around

Trout Lake, and something would have to be done about it sooner or later. When railroadman Paul Price of Whitefish, Montana, lost a string of cutthroat trout to the bear and was chased halfway around the lakeshore, he wound up telling his story to a ranger who almost seemed bored by the news. "That bear's been chasing people all summer," the ranger said, "and a little last summer."

"What are you gonna do when it catches somebody?" Price asked.

"Well, I don't know," the ranger said bemusedly. "He hasn't caught anybody yet."

By the middle of the summer, Glacier Park was sweltering. Day after day, new record-high temperatures were posted at the weather station, and the glaciers from which the park derived its name had long since lost their outer coatings of fresh snow; now they were a uniformly dirty white. The rocky ground of the whole park had become thirsty. The Weeping Wall was barely dripping, and at least once a day someone could be counted on to say that the Weeping Wall soon would be down to a mere frown. The splash and spatter of Birdwoman Falls no longer was heard; only a trickle of water passed over its rim. Fires broke out, and the surveillance had to be increased sharply. Smoke jumpers were called out frequently, and crews of Indians were recruited to beat back small blazes that threatened tens of thousands of heavily forested acres.

The hot and unpleasant month of July was almost over when two 14-year-old schoolboy chums, John Cook and Steve Ashlock, packed into Trout Lake for a three-day festival of fishing, and hardly had the boys set up camp when a fire broke out on the ridge to the west, and they were treated to the thrilling sight of ten smoke jumpers arriving to put out the blaze. They also were treated to the thrilling sight of five or six bears, blacks and grizzlies both, coming to the lake for water, and the boys guessed that the general drought in the park had dried up some of the springs back in the hills. There was a light rain on the day they arrived, but it quit after about three minutes, and soon the bright sun was beating back down on them. They caught a few cutthroats, cooked them at their campsite alongside the logjam, and turned in early.

The next day, the two young boys from nearby Columbia Falls, Montana, were exploring the logjam, trying to find a way across, when they heard a noise from their camp behind them and turned to see a dark, skinny grizzly sitting on its haunches eating a loaf of their bread. Both Steve and John knew that grizzlies would run from humans, so they crept to within 10 to 15 feet of the animal and began yelling. The bear looked them over coldly and kept on eating. The boys picked up some small stones and began pelting the animal, whereupon the bear reared up and scuttled to a log a few feet closer to them and began growling. "Get out of here!" Steve hollered, but the bear only growled louder. The boys resumed throwing, this time with heavier rocks, and when one of them caught the grizzly in the leg, it bolted out of the camp like an excited racehorse, circled around a few times, and then returned and began ripping at the canvas packs.

Now that they could see how fast the big animal could move and how powerful were its jaws, the two boys retreated once again to the middle of the logjam. They figured that the bear would not stay long, and it would be safer simply to wait quietly. From their vantage point, they watched as the animal slashed their packs into small pieces and bent the frames. Then it strolled to the lakeside for a drink and came across a pan containing ten cleaned trout, the boys' dinner. After gobbling up the fish, the bear walked out on the logjam, its head twisting for scent. The boys retreated to the place where the heavy logs petered out and there was nothing but a channel of cold lake water. Now the bear stopped, distracted by the remains of a smelly trout that had been lying in the sun on one of the logs. The boys decided to take to the water and try to swim around the grizzly to the eastern shore above the campsite. But as they were taking their boots off, they remembered that bears were good swimmers, so they decided to ease themselves into the lake, swim underwater to a point beneath the logs, and lie there with only their noses poking up for air. They had just begun to carry out this last-ditch escape plan when the bear tossed the remains of the sunbaked trout into the air and headed at a brisk pace back to the campsite, as though it had suddenly decided that it did not have to eat garbage when there was fresh food around.

Steve and John grabbed their boots and began lacing them back on, while the bear tore wildly at their camp. They crept across the logjam toward the animal, and when they were within 25 or 30 feet, they stepped into the shallow water and waded to the bushes on the opposite edge of the logjam from the bear. They ran about 100 feet down Camas Creek and then cut through the dense vegetation and headed for the trail that wound over Howe Ridge to the Lake McDonald ranger station. In one hour, the panting youngsters covered four miles, including a 1,500-foot climb and a corresponding 2,000-foot descent, and burst out on the road shortly after ten at night. A ranger heard their story and advised them to wait till morning to go back and recover the remains of their equipment. He said that the bear had been bothering people all summer and that he was planning to do something about it.

Steve and John spent the night in a nearby cabin and returned to Trout Lake in the morning. They found wreckage littered in a wide circle, and one of the packs had been dragged along the trail and into the woods to a hole in the ground about 40 feet up the hillside. Their Coleman lantern had been punctured, and the fuel had run out. Spaghetti and chili cans were crushed and torn, and two flip-top cans of Vienna sausages had been opened exactly according to the instructions and devoured. A pair of leather boots lay to one side; the uppers were scarred with teeth marks, and the tongues had been ripped away. The boys' light-green tent was ripped and ruined. They gathered what they could and went home.

A few days later, an official report appeared in the park records. It read: 7-29-67. Steve Ashlock, John Cook, two torn packs, torn shoe, torn tent, ate all food. Dollar value of damage $30. No action taken. Backcountry incident."

On August 4, there was a brief item in the weekly *Hungry Horse News*. Under the headline "ENCOUNTER BEAR AT 'TROUT LAKE," the newspaper noted that Steve Ashlock and John Cook of Columbia Falls were the "latest" to meet the Trout Lake bear and told the tale of their narrow escape. There was no response from ranger headquarters. Later, much later, a high park official was to comment that somebody should have called the article to his attention.

—3—

THAT SUMMER: GRANITE PARK

Eight or nine crow-flight miles from Trout Lake, but separated from it by the 9,000-foot cliffs and spires of the Livingstone Range, a stark and colorless mountain chalet hunkers down against the winds and snows of winter and opens its doors for guests only two months of the year. The place is called Granite Park Chalet, and it stands at the confluence of several busy footpaths, which lead like the spokes of a wheel in all directions. Four miles down one of the trails, at the bottom of a long series of steep switchbacks, is Going-to-the-Sun Highway; that is the closest one can get to the chalet on anything but foot or horseback.

The bulky old building has endured a half century of winter's buffetings; by January or February of each year, it is usually all but buried under snow and ice, and the last patch does not melt away until July or sometimes August. But in the short warmth of summertime, the chalet lies in spectacular surroundings, like a speck of common sandstone set in a ring of diamonds and rubies. The building itself is nothing more than an oversized blockhouse, an inflated version of a Swiss mountain hut. Except for a few additions and small outbuildings, the structure is a 48-foot square, two stories tall, with a heavily timbered roof and fieldstone sides. The chalet lies just below timberline, 6,600 feet, in an area where trees and brush and flowers lead an ephemeral existence. The mountainside is like some of the deserts of the Southwest, drab and almost without color for nine or ten months of the year, and covered with a brilliant carpet of flowers in the summer. The broad bench just below the chalet bursts into bloom in July and August; out of the rocky soil grow alpine buttercups, monkey flowers, and harebells, the true bluebells-of-Scotland. The delicate alpine saxifrage, a tiny flower that grows in mountains all over the world, almost seems to pop from the surface of rocks. Farther down on the bench, bear grass grows five feet tall, and one finds mountain sweet cinque-foil, Indian paintbrush, acres of false hellebores and glacier lilies, and wide patches of lavender asters, dainty and frangible. Above the chalet, a twisting trail leads through stands of miniature subalpine firs, and the shortest side trip by the hiker will turn up medallions of heliotrope, alpine erigerons, carpet pink, heather, and the white-flowered member of the rose family, the Mt. Washington dryad.

Two tiny streams water the area, and despite the inhospitality of the frigid winds that slash across the mountainside like giant scythes, a few berry bushes manage to survive, and there are scattered trees, their branches reaching out on the lee side, their windward side bare. The limber pine grows in a few places around the chalet, its thinner branches twisted into knots by the high winds. The most common tree is the subalpine fir, but here at timberline it seldom reaches more than eight or ten feet in height. Its sap smells like balsam, and some believe it is antiseptic. Here and there, a tree has fallen and rotted into the stony ground, leaving only a shadow, a trunk print, lying flat and two-dimensional like a big dress pattern. Other dead trees, branchless trunks, cling to verticality, their bark shredded and ripped by the pileated woodpeckers that throw up clouds of chips and splinters like housewreckers. Someday these bare trunks, called snags, will crash to the ground and create their own trunk prints, and it will be decades before trees of similar size can form as replacements. They will grow up slowly, a few inches per year, their branches reaching out toward the sun that is always in the south, their roots groping for a grip in the rocky soil that permits only the shallowest penetration.

Millions of years before, when Glacier Park and all of North America were under the seas, a mass of molten lava squirted out of the ocean floor and congealed into a vast ledge of basalt, and now this slab of dark rock, ranging in thickness from 50 to 275 feet, reaches for hundreds of yards around the chalet. The fine-grained basalt is the reason for the misnomer "Granite" Park. To old-time prospectors, almost every igneous rock was granite, whether it was light in color like true granite or gray-black like the basalt of this mountainside. Here and there, spatters of green- and yellow- and orange-colored lichens have succeeded in breaking down portions of the rocky slab, and miniature trees and bushes keep trying to establish homesteads in the new soil thus created, but they are seldom able to achieve a height of more than a foot or two; they are dwarfs consigned to dwarfism for at least a few more centuries.

In this timberline setting, several species of fauna somehow manage to thrive. Columbian ground squirrels are common, and occasionally one sees a golden-mantled ground squirrel. Marmots whistle at intruders, and every year or two one of the mischievous beaver-sized animals will allow itself to be perverted into hanging around the chalet, taking handouts, and the local newspapers will scurry up and shoot pictures. Higher on the steep mountainside, up toward the 7,200-foot Swiftcurrent Pass, mountain goats gambol about, and deer browse on almost nothing, seeming to find the thin slivers of vegetation as delicious as they are minuscule. Now and then, an elk will shoulder its way through the region, but the big-antlered animals are not common here. Of the larger mammals, only the grizzly appears with absolute regularity. The bench just below the chalet is alive with some of the *pieces de resistance* of the grizzly cuisine, and in certain seasons of the year, the soil of the bench is pockmarked from the busy, nocturnal diggings of the hungry bears. In the middle of this ursine happy hunting ground, the government has established a public campground. It is used by an occasional visitor to the park, but seldom by rangers.

When Tom Walton and his wife, Nancy, accepted the summertime job at Granite Park Chalet, they had only the vaguest idea of what they were doing. The only certainties were that they had some time off between semesters, and the pay was not bad, and they needed to lay up a few dollars for the next year when Tom would be working on his master's degree at the University of Denver. For four previous summers, the 23-year-old Walton had worked as a firefighter, but this new opening at the remote and isolated Granite Park Chalet would offer him and his wife twenty-four hours of daily togetherness, minus the dangers that came from roaring fires. So they accepted, and late in June, 1967, they found themselves picking their way up the snowy trail on horseback. The chalet was half-buried in drifts, even at this late date, but they were surprised to find no grizzly tracks. One of the ranger executives at headquarters had told them that he had made a few flights over the chalet earlier in the spring, and there had always been grizzlies around, and once he had seen six on the chalet roof. Walton, a gentle person despite his fireplug build and his experience as a football lineman, was just as glad.

For several days, they worked almost around the clock, readying the chalet that they would help to manage all summer, along with Mrs. Eileen Anderson. The Waltons would take care of the guests, and Mrs. Anderson, a middle-aged woman from Minnesota, would boss a crew of girls who attended to everything else: the kitchen work, the bed making, and the general housekeeping. It fell to Tom Walton, as the only man on the premises, to dig out the water system; it lay under five feet of snow and took him the better part of a day to reach. It also fell to him to fire up a small incinerator that the Park Service had installed for burning garbage, but only a few trials with the gadget showed the young Walton that someone had bought the wrong size. The incinerator would barely burn away the garbage of the eight or ten members of the chalet staff, and Walton told his wife that as soon as the guests began arriving they would have to figure out another system. They had been told to avoid dumping too much garbage out in the gully behind the chalet, because that would attract grizzlies, and grizzlies would be dangerous to the guests.

The young couple had given little thought to the big bears in the general busyness of their first two or three days in the lonely place. Everyone had told them that they would see grizzlies galore during the summer; indeed, grizzlies were the main attraction at the chalet, and everybody for miles around knew it. When tourists would check in at the visitors' centers at St. Mary and Rising Sun and Logan Pass and the ranger headquarters on the west side, they would soon find out that the most exciting trip in the park was the one to Granite Park Chalet to see the grizzlies.

But after several days, the Waltons began to wonder, and a few veteran members of the housekeeping staff, mostly young girls, began to worry. "Tom," one of them said one night, "we haven't even seen a sign of a bear. Maybe they're not gonna show up this summer."

"Oh, that would be awful!" said another. "They're our main drawing card."

Drawing card or not, the bears could take their time so far as Tom Walton was concerned. He was not in terror of the big animals, but he entertained no illusions about them, either. Walton was a native of Idaho; he had been stomping around grizzly woods all his life and listening to tales about the great beasts, and while he knew that they were relatively harmless, he also knew that the house was four miles from the nearest road and had absolutely no medical facilities and not so much as a twenty-gauge shotgun to drive rogue animals away.

By the third night, the chalet staff was intact, and everything was in readiness for the guests, who would begin arriving shortly after the official opening on July 1. It was nearly midnight; two of the girls were sitting around downstairs drinking a final cup of coffee, and the Waltons were almost asleep in their room just above, when the door to the outside began banging and a very annoyed Tom Walton climbed out of bed in his boxer shorts to secure the lock. He opened the door momentarily and flicked his flashlight beam down the back stairs and picked up the bright-orange eyes of a big animal. He realized that he was looking at a grizzly, standing on top of a snowdrift not twenty feet away, and he slammed the door and locked it. "Don't go out there!" he shouted through the cracks in the floor. "There's a grizzly outside." The girls jumped up, ran out the back door, and began searching for the animal. Luckily it had fled. Trying to get back to sleep upstairs, Tom Walton wondered what would possess a person to walk out into the snows of midnight to try to get a close-up glimpse of a monstrous terrestrial beast of prey.

For the next few nights, grizzlies would arrive, sniff around the chalet while everyone was asleep, and be gone by the next morning. The Waltons were fascinated by their tracks, especially the persistent track of an adult with cubs. Every morning, they would see the same signs, but no matter how late they stayed up at the darkened windows, bear watching, they could see nothing. Wearily they would turn in, and the next morning the tracks of mother and young would be clearly marked in the packed drifts. Once the couple mixed up a batter of plaster and water and tried to make a cast in the snow, but the process did not work. Soon there were so many tracks that one would lap over another as though the animals had been staging sprint contests around and around the chalet in the small hours of night, and every morning the Waltons would find tracks running right up to the front door. A couple of old hands explained to the Waltons that the big bears had been coming to Granite Park for years to clean up on table scraps, and that they were probably chasing around the chalet at night wondering where their regular handouts were.

By the end of the first week of July, regular guests were arriving, and the crew of the mountainside resort was settling into a routine, but not without complications. There were a few cases of cabin fever, mostly after still, breezeless nights, when the young girls would have to face something that few Americans had encountered: total silence, not the silence that comes to the city dweller when he goes to bed at night against an unnoticed drone of automobile engines and generators and house noises and the million ordinary sounds of civilization, but the absolute, utter silence of the wilderness. Even the Waltons were disturbed at first by the stillness; lying in their bed at night, they could almost feel the heaviness of the quiet air, and they found themselves hoping for a light breeze, or the howl of a coyote, or even a honk from an automobile on the Going-to-the-Sun Highway four miles distant. Nobody was surprised when one of the sturdy young girls of the kitchen staff took off one morning, hiked seven miles to Logan Pass on the Highline Trail, hitchhiked to Many Glacier, and then walked twelve miles over Swiftcurrent Pass and back to Granite Park. "Now I feel better," she said, and everyone understood.

∞

By the middle of July, the hot summer sun had sliced several feet off the snowdrifts around Granite Park Chalet, and soon the trails were completely clear and visitors were arriving by the dozens. Mrs. Anderson, a stickler for cleanliness, was frantic about the garbage. Each night there was more of it, and the little incinerator could no longer handle the load. Tom Walton punched holes in the side of a fifty-gallon drum and tried to burn garbage that way, but each morning he would go outside and find that the bears had arrived and knocked over the drum to dine on the unburned residue. He talked the problem over with Mrs. Anderson and their boss, concessioner Ross Luding, and soon the garbage was being handled in the old manner. About fifty yards back of the chalet, across a shallow gully and up on the side of a hill, there was a cleared place in the weeds that marked where leftovers had been placed in the past, and each night all the garbage would be put in a pail and carried out to the spot. As though they had been waiting in the wings for their cues, the bears began to show up regularly just after dark. For a while, the dramatis personae changed from week to week, and the Waltons suspected that they were being visited by nomadic bears that had just left hibernation and were still on the road. Two small buckskin-colored grizzlies stayed around for a few days, but they soon gave way to others, and in those middle weeks of July there was only one constant: Each morning, there would be the fresh tracks of a big bear and two cubs.

Then, for a few days, a consistent pattern seemed to develop. A large buckskin grizzly and an equally large dark bear would slowly walk up the narrow trail along the lava flow and begin to pick at the food with great dignity shortly after dark. While they were dining, sometimes backing off to woof and threaten each other, a small light-colored bear would run at top speed straight up the draw that led from the campground below and catapult itself into the garbage area like a character out of the animated cartoons. Invariably, the smaller bear would meet the same fate: One of the others would knock him flat on his back with a single swipe. Squealing and screeching, the small bear would usually run back down the draw at the same high speed, but now and then it would simply move off a few feet, lie in the snow, and watch till the two big bears had eaten their fill. Then it would rush into the dump, grab a few scraps, and disappear down the draw toward the Granite Park campground.

For a time, the arrivals and departures of the three bears were so regular that Walton and the chalet employees were able to amaze the guests with their knowledge of the animals' habits. "The bears will arrive in exactly ten minutes," Walton would say, and ten minutes later the first animal would be heard huffing and puffing up the trail. Word of the remarkable bear show had spread around the tourist centers, and soon the chalet was groaning with sixty and sixty-five guests every night, absolute capacity. There were daily hikes from Logan Pass, led by ranger-naturalists; the parties would walk the scenic seven-mile trail along the Continental Divide and arrive at Granite Park Chalet, footsore and weary. After dinner, the revitalized visitors would sit in the chalet's main dining room while the naturalist gave a short talk on his own specialty, flowers or birds or mammals or some other subject, and then the giddiness of high altitude would set in, and the dudes would sing songs like "I've Been Working on the Railroad." Almost without fail, Tom Walton or one of the chalet employees would arrive in the middle of the third or fourth song and make the announcement about the bears, and sixty or seventy people would run outside to watch the animals growl and frolic and enjoy their evening repasts not fifty yards away. Walton soon learned from longtime visitors to the place that such bear shows had been going on nightly at Granite Park Chalet for decades; in fact, grizzlies were the chalet's claim to fame, just as mountain goats were the main attraction at Sperry Chalet, a few miles away.

One evening, the slop in the garbage pail included two pounds of spoiled bacon, and that night Walton noticed that two big bears squared off in a knockdown fight, complete with loud grunts and ferocious swings and several near-decapitations. The guests clapped and applauded, and a few of them tried to creep down the gully to get closer to the grizzlies for pictures, but Walton quickly grabbed them and told them they were endangering their health. He found one man who had hidden behind a tree near the bears and ordered him back to the safety of the chalet.

After the night of the first big fight, Walton heard that any delicacy like a slab of spoiled bacon or a ham rind would cause the big animals to circle and threaten each other and sometimes trade blows, and since this seemed to go over big with the tourists and the bears did not seem to be concerned about anything but themselves, he was not worried. Once or twice, when the bears had been acting too docile to stir up the crowds, Walton slipped a few pieces of bacon into the pail, and the bears reacted by fighting. One night, in fact, the battle broke out again after all the visitors had gone to bed, and for several hours the screams and growls continued intermittently in the night. The ranger-naturalist who had led that afternoon's hike managed to sleep through all the noise, and a few days later he was ordered by park headquarters to provide a full report on "the bear fight at Granite Park." The chagrined ranger came back to Walton for a fill-in, and when Walton asked how park headquarters had found out about the incident, the ranger told him, "It filtered back. Everything that happens up here filters back." Walton guessed that the park had a complete dossier on every event of the summer, including the abandonment of the faulty incinerator and the resumption of the nightly feeding schedule, but he did not see any reason to worry. Six or seven ranger-naturalists had regularly watched the bears feed, and several other rangers, including a few executives, had spent the night at the chalet and witnessed the ritual, and only one person had expressed the slightest hint of criticism. A high official of the park had said, "Tom, don't you feed those bears anymore."

"OK," Walton said.

"And you better start burning all your garbage in the incinerator we got for you," the ranger executive said.

Rather than argue, Walton nodded agreeably, but later that night he told his wife that the instructions did not sound serious to him, that he was willing to bet that this particular ranger official enjoyed watching the feeding bears as much as anyone and was merely going through the motions of admonishing him. He discussed the matter with Ross Luding, and the veteran concessioner told him that there was nothing to worry about, to continue putting out the scraps. "It's against the rules," Luding said, "but I don't know what else to do, and neither does the Park Service."

∞

By early August, the Granite Park Chalet's official two-month season was half over, and the grizzlies' visits to the garbage dump had become a big talking point in the park, but the Park Service's public position was that animal feeding was strongly prohibited by several dozen rules and regulations, and therefore it must not be going on. Rangers and naturalists who took in the nightly display of grizzlies went along with their superiors; most of the rangers had filed protests, written or verbal, at one time or another, to one executive or another, but when they saw that the ritual appeared as inevitable as the nightly singing of "I've been Working on the Railroad," they said nothing more. High park officials would deny that so much as a single scrap of food was being put out for wild animals anywhere in the park. If such illegal activities were going on, they said, they would be the first to know about it.

As the deep snows melted off in the harsh sun of this abnormally hot summer, all trails were cleared and hikers began arriving in record numbers, many of them taking advantage of the chalet's bargain rates: $12.50 for a cot and three square meals. Some nights, every bed would be taken, and eight or ten more customers would stretch out on the floor in their sleeping bags. If there had ever been a sliver of a chance that the small incinerator could handle the leftovers, it was gone now. Tom Walton had a slop bucket for the garbage, and in the beginning of the season it had never been completely full. Now it was brimming to the top routinely, and sometimes he would have to dump it and come back for more. With such lavish fare, the bears had become a permanent fixture. Looking back on the summer later, Walton realized why some authorities said that grizzlies were creatures of habit. From mid-July until the chalet closed after Labor Day, the bears had arrived almost every night.

But this familiarity with grizzlies did not delude the young innkeeper into underestimating the animals, as certain others did. When hikers would arrive and announce their intention of sleeping on the ground in the Granite Park campground below, Walton would give them his standard lecture on grizzlies, closing with the suggestion that bears were always unpredictable. He advised long-distance hikers to carry bear bells, so that they would not take the bears by surprise, and if they had no bells, he would improvise them out of tin cans and iron washers and tie them to the backpacks.

By now, the domestic staff of the timberline inn had cured its outbreaks of cabin fever and settled into a regular routine, and a few of the girls were even enjoying summer romances, though at a certain nightly risk. About 500 yards down the trail that wended along the lower edge of the lava flow, the Park Service had built a small cabin out of logs and corrugated metal, and each night two girls from the chalet would rush to finish their duties so they could hike to the cabin and visit the young trail workers in residence. The girls used the same path frequented by grizzlies on their own nightly trips to the chalet. Usually, the two girls would head toward the trail cabin while the bears were at the dump, but sometimes their work would tie them up longer, and they would follow the bears back down the trail. The situation disturbed Tom Walton, and when his own warnings to the girls seemed to have no effect, he took the matter up with concessioner Luding. The older man was highly popular with his employees; his manner tended to be light and jocular, but this time he laid down the law to the two girls. He told them that grizzlies make poor nocturnal companions, and that no summer romance was worth such a risk. The girls promised to visit their boyfriends at other hours, but soon they resumed their trips just as though nothing had been said. By 9 or 9:30 p.m., they would be gone, and an hour or two later, the trail workers would bring them back by the light of lanterns. Tom Walton threw up his hands; there was a limit to how much advice one could hand out without becoming a bore, and he felt he had reached the limit.

But one night, a seasonal naturalist and wintertime schoolteacher found out about the romantic activities and was aghast. "My God, man," he said to Walton, "don't you realize that those girls are sharing a path with grizzlies?"

Walton said he realized it fully.

"Well, you just can't let them do it!" the naturalist said. "Now you've just got to go and tell them to quit! "

Wearily, Walton said he would tell the girls, and he did, but again nothing changed. The innkeeper consoled himself with the fact that the bears' behavior had seemed to become more consistent as July had turned to August. There were two of them now, regular nightly visitors, although tracks and other signs indicated that a sow and a pair of cubs were coming in late at night, long after the chalet was asleep. The two "regular" bears had learned to live with the powerful flashlights that were shone on them and the monotone of awed conversation that came from the chalet 150 feet away, where a throng of guests watched in hushed excitement. Some nights, the two bears would stay for as long as thirty minutes, taking turns eating, circling each other, dipping in and out of the tree cover behind the dump, and now and then having a minor disagreement.

Walton and the chalet staff had not gone to the extreme of

naming the bears, as others had done in the past. They were
called simply No. 1 and No. 2. No. 1 was a big silvertip, a
handsome animal with dark-brown fur and extreme dignity.
Sometimes the flashlights would catch No. 1 just right, and its
fur would take on a ghostly luminescence, and an admiring
gasp would come from the onlookers. Naturalists guessed the
big bear's weight at 500 pounds.

No. 2 was a smaller grizzly with a shoddy coat and long
claws. Wildlife experts in the crowd would explain to the tenderfeet that such claws were a sign that the bear had given up
its normal ways of finding food, such as digging for glacier lily
bulbs and Columbian ground squirrels, and was depending on
man for most of its sustenance. Probably the bear was old, with
worn teeth; certainly it was crotchety, and it soon was playing
the nightly role of villain in the little backyard tableaux. No.
1 would arrive from the direction of the trail cabin just after
dark, and a few minutes later, No. 2 would come up the same
path and start the trouble. Sometimes the massive silvertip
would see the grouchy bear coming and simply move into the
brush to wait. Then No. 2 would stuff itself with garbage and
leave by the same route. There were a few nights when No. 1
would stand its ground at the dump when the mangier bear
arrived, and the two would circle and growl and woof at each
other and finally come to blows, but in a few seconds, No. 1
would disengage itself from the undignified proceedings and
walk slowly to the trees to wait. It was plain to everyone that
No. 1 could have vanquished the smaller bear at any time,
but the naturalists explained that there was something called
the peck order, and somehow or other the smaller bear had
achieved ascendancy over the silvertip. The crowds, being ac-
customed to movies and television, could not understand why
the handsome hero always lost and the runty villain always
won in these nightly encounters, and some of the chalet staff
joined them in hoping for the smaller bear's downfall.

One night, No. 1 was eating peacefully, bathed in the light

of two high-powered flashlights focused from the chalet, when No. 2 came up the trail and walked straight to the food. This was usually No. 1's cue to depart, but this time the big animal stood its ground, and the aggressive smaller bear moved in to fight. Instantly, the silvertip clamped its mouth on the smaller bear's head, and with a massive display of strength flipped the other bear into the air and down on its back. The crowd cheered and applauded, and Tom Walton felt himself sharing the enthusiasm. But then the big bear started walking off to the trees as though it had lost. "Come back!" Walton wanted to holler, "Come back! You won, stupid! You've got the food now!" but he restrained himself. The smaller bear pulled itself together and began dining as though nothing had happened, while the silvertip waited its turn patiently. The peck order remained unchanged.

—4—

THE LAST WEEK

By the beginning of August, 1967, Glacier Park was in the middle of its most hectic season. The summer was unnaturally hot everywhere; visitors were coming from all over to sit on glacial ice and turn their noses into the alpine winds and walk under mantles of conifers that would shield them from the sun. But even in Glacier Park, the summer remained scaldingly hot. Temperatures of 90 degrees were commonplace, and rangers were learning to accustom themselves to carping tourists who complained that they should have stayed in Indianapolis or Fort Worth or Drexel Hill, Pennsylvania, as though somehow the Park Service had cheated them by falsely promising an air-conditioned paradise. To worsen the situation, headquarters' rangers frequently found themselves called from their normal duties to battle the persistent fires that broke out in the dry brush. The Park Service personnel were stretched thinner and thinner, and only a handful of skilled men were left to handle the record crowds. In such an atmosphere, no one had time to keep track of bears, either black or grizzly, much less to keep records on the increasing numbers of face-to-face meetings between grizzlies and man, particularly at the remote places called Granite Park and Trout Lake. While no one was noticing, the contacts between man and bear were reaching the point where something had to give.

Early in the second week of August, a droll personage named Izzy Kolodejchuk checked out a horse and headed up the trail toward Swiftcurrent Lookout, just above Granite Park Chalet on the edge of the Continental Divide. Izzy was an electronic technician assigned to service radios, and he was a welcome sight at the park's lonely outposts. For one thing, Izzy was always good for a laugh; he had learned to enjoy the constant kidding about his long, Polish name. "Kolodejchuk," he would say. "Ko-lo-day-chuck: The J is silent, like the P in swimming." Izzy had been brought up on a ranch in North Dakota, and horses were a way of life to him, but grizzlies were not. He had never seen a grizzly, and in the hectic activity of this first summer in Glacier Park, he had heard little about them. Mostly he had worked and told jokes and laughed about his name.

The radio at Swiftcurrent posed no major problems; Izzy reached into his saddlebags and pulled out a few parts and made it as good as new. Then he remounted his horse and rode back down through a light rain to Granite Park Chalet, where already the standing-room-only sign had been posted. The young innkeeper, Tom Walton, said he could squeeze the park employee in, and Izzy went outside and hitched his horse to a rail in the back of the chalet. It was nearly dark, and he was just sitting down in the dining room when he heard someone shout, "The bears! The bears are here! "

Izzy blurted out to no one in particular, "What bears?" and someone answered, "The grizzlies!"

Izzy jumped up and ran to the back of the chalet, where already thirty or forty guests milled about excitedly. But the radio technician was a North Dakotan, and instead of gawking at the bear that was dimly visible on the other side of the shallow gully, he looked toward his horse. The animal was keening in the direction of the bears, and Izzy saw that it was shuffling its feet and acting highly nervous. Now another bear had come on the scene, and the horse began pulling hard at its tether. One thought passed through the technician's head—that the saddlebags were full of antennae and other heavy equipment, and if the horse ran away, he would have to haul the stuff out himself. Immediately, Izzy picked up a rock and threw it toward the bears, but the range was too long, and the shadowy animals made no move to leave. He cupped his hands and began to whistle and holler. "Get out!" he said. "Beat it! Hey, bears!" He noticed that a few members of the chalet staff were looking at him oddly, but he was in the green uniform of a park employee and nobody stopped him. In fact, nobody spoke to him at all until he took a few steps down the gully to shorten the range and then he was told, "Watch your step! Don't get too close!" Izzy threw a few more rocks and returned to comfort his horse till the bears left in their own time. Just before the larger of the bears wandered back down the trail and the last guest went inside the chalet, Izzy heard someone humming. He turned to see a young light-haired girl strolling down the path, carrying a guitar and a pie. "Girl," Izzy shouted, "you crazy?" The girl turned and smiled and kept on going.

A night or two later, a party of four headed toward Granite Park to see if all the rumors were true. For weeks, the members of this party had been hearing that genuine, live grizzly bears were making nightly appearances at the chalet, and since grizzly bears were among the most exciting and interesting of the carnivores, they were going in to see for themselves. The hikers were not much different from the hundreds of others who had been walking to Granite Park to ogle bears, except that two of them were in ranger uniforms. Bert Gildart, a 27-year-old seasonal ranger, was with his wife, Margie; and Dave Shea, a

21-year-old assistant park biologist, was with Roberta Seibel, curator of the park's museum at headquarters. The two men had worked that day, but their curiosity about the bears was so intense that they led the women up the tortuous trail at the end of their regular shifts. At the chalet, they were told that two bears had been coming in every night, and that the tracks of another adult bear with cubs frequently were seen around the garbage dump in the morning.

On this night, the big silvertip was the first to arrive, shortly after 10 o'clock, and a few minutes later, a smaller bear moved in and chased the other into the brush line. When both bears had fed, the four visitors went inside for a cup of coffee. Activities in the chalet were coming to a halt: hikers were tired and going off to bed; the kitchen crew finished cleaning up and disappeared into closed rooms, and soon there was almost no one up and around but Gildart and Shea and the two young women. Just before midnight, they walked quietly out the front door to begin the return trip down the Alder Trail, and as they turned around the edge of the big building, they heard woofing noises from the garbage pit. They slipped around to the back and saw a large bear and two cubs dining peacefully on leftover leftovers.

On the way down the trail, Gildart and Shea talked about their mammal-watching coup: five grizzlies in a single night, a lifetime's supply for most observers. But the young men were not exhilarated. Shea was annoyed because he knew about the incinerator and the park's efforts to eliminate the unnatural food supply, and now he had seen with his own eyes that the bear feeding was worse than ever. Gildart was annoyed because he believed thoroughly in the park's reason for existence–to show nature in natural settings. Glacier National Park was not a zoo.

But neither man made any official report, and in fact they almost avoided talking about what they had seen: It seemed to them that they were just about the last to be let in on the "secret," and they realized that they had been naive to doubt the stories that had been trickling down all summer from the lonely old chalet. Briefly, they worried about the location of the Granite Park campground below the chalet; they had seen bears come from the direction of the camping area and return in the same direction, but they made no report on this matter, either. Wise, experienced heads had established the campsite in the middle of the bear's stamping grounds; surely there must have been good reason. The two young men had mildly disturbing thoughts, but they did nothing.

Toward the end of the week, Granite Park Chalet was visited by another man in ranger green, Francis Elmore, the great park's chief naturalist, accompanied by a distinguished guest, Mr. A. J. Taylor of Santa Fe, New Mexico, a businessman and brother-in-law of President Lyndon Johnson. Ladybird Johnson's brother had been visiting Elmore and the park for several days, and the two old friends agreed to make the four-mile uphill hike to Granite Park together. The walk took the middle-aged men a little longer than expected, with botanist Elmore stopping frequently to deliver impromptu and enlightening lectures on the park's flora, but the party reached the chalet in plenty of time for the big attraction: grizzlies.

It was not long before A. J. Taylor of Santa Fe, New Mexico, was feeling exceedingly nervous. Although he talked and joked and laughed with the sixty or sixty-five others who waited in the rear of the chalet for the animals to appear, his mind was full of forebodings about grizzlies. With the arrival of the first bear at the pit, some fifty yards away, the president's brother-in-law sneaked a peek over his shoulder to see if it would be possible to climb on the roof. He decided that it would be possible, but most likely the younger people would beat him to it. He asked one of the rangers if there were any guns in the chalet, and he was told with a certain coolness that guns were absolutely forbidden in the park. "I was indignant!" he told friends later. "Absolutely indignant! I thought, The park people are so dedicated to preserving the wildlife that they aren't even protecting the people. Why, a bear could have gone berserk and massacred everyone there! "

A large, silvertip bear had been enjoying itself at the garbage dump for several minutes when Taylor and his companions began to hear sounds from the trail below the gully. "It's the other bear," someone whispered, but someone else said quickly, "Not unless he's wearing bear bells." Sure enough, whatever was headed up the trail was making a steady, rhythmical tinkle and hallooing loudly. "My God," cried one of the rangers, "it's somebody hiking in!" The ranger ran to the side of the balcony and shouted, "Leave the trail! The bear's here! Get off the trail and come up in a direct line through the brush!"

A few minutes later, two badly frightened teenage boys burst into the front door. Taylor heard them explain that they had been hiking and had seen another bear a few hundred yards below, and they had rushed up the trail toward the chalet, thinking it would be the last place where grizzlies would be found. They said that they had intended to sleep out overnight in the campground just below, but now they were too scared. One of the chalet employees offered them flashlights to guide their way, but the two boys asked if they could roll out their sleeping bags on the dining-room floor. The place was booked solid, but room was found for the refugees alongside the front door.

In this final week of relative normalcy in Glacier National Park, Trout Lake was proportionately just as overcrowded with people and grizzlies as Granite Park Chalet. On a normal summer weekday, there might be a party or two fishing in the cool waters of the mile-square lake, but there might also be no one but bears and otters on the scene. Guided tours were not conducted into Trout Lake as they were into Granite Park, and there was no chalet to provide a roof against summer storms. Usually, it was only the genuine, bona fide hikers and fishermen who made the trip, and there seldom were enough of these to overcrowd the sylvan setting.

But this long, hot summer was different. People were beating their way over the 2,000-foot Howe Ridge in great numbers, and their debris was to be seen all around the lakeshore. Groups would come streaming down the mountainside toward the campsite, only to see smoke curling upward, and then they would hike two more miles up the trail to the shelter cabin to the north and discover that it was occupied, and they would end up pitching camp somewhere in the open. Trail registers were full of complaints and remarks about the situation, but the registers were just as jammed as the park, and now there was no more space for entries.

On the afternoon of Tuesday, August 8, 1967, a pleasant young school-teaching couple named Chase guided the girls of Scout Troop 367, Kalispell, Montana, into this less-than-idyllic setting for what was scheduled to be a three-day camping trip. The hike had been enjoyed by all; most of the dirty hauling work was done by Jerry Chase's little gray pony, Sage, and this had freed the six young girls from the heaviest loads. They were still laughing and joking and having a happy time when they came to the trail register a few hundred feet from the lake and read the last entry: "Caught 15 beautiful trout and lost them to bear." Jerry Chase and his wife Sharon noticed that at least half the entries on the register mentioned bears, but they were not worried; they were veterans at hiking in Glacier Park, and they doubted that there was a bear alive that would come near a camp full of giggly, noisy girls. But they had momentary second thoughts when they arrived at the campsite along the logjam. To Chase, the place looked like a battlefield strewn with K rations. Tin cans had been bitten in half and packs shredded and a pair of blue jeans ripped into tatters and cans of corn and spaghetti punctured and drained. Above the trail, in a depression dug into the humus beneath a spruce tree, there was a pile of trash, most of it damaged the same as the material in the campsite. Both Chases made mental notes to keep a wary eye out for bears, but they did not communicate their fears to the happy young girls. Anyway, there was little time to be afraid. There was a camp to be laid, fish to be caught, and dinner to be cooked and served.

Susie Sampson, a 13-year-old from Kalispell, borrowed a metal lure from Chase and went off and caught herself an eight-inch cutthroat trout, which she proudly carried back into camp with all the braggadocio of a successful marlin fisherman. There were still two hours of daylight after dinner, and all the provisions were tied into a canvas sack and hauled high into a tree. Then the host and hostess and six Girl Scouts and one weary gray pony hiked a mile to the deep upper end of the lake for some more fishing. On the way back, darkness was falling, there was fresh bear sign on the trail, and the girls quickly became frightened. "Don't worry," Sharon Chase said. "We'll just sing to scare them away." All the way back to camp the girls sang songs like "The Ballad of the Green Berets" and school songs from Kalispell, and Mr. and Mrs. Jerry Chase found themselves making as much noise as the children. In lifetimes of hiking in and out of grizzly zones, neither of the Chases had ever seen so much indication that bears were about or such clear evidence that bears had been visiting camps with impunity.

The night was clear, and every star in the heavens made a gaudy, personal appearance. Before turning in, the girls popped corn over an open fire, and in this inexact process, they charred some of it beyond edibility. They ate what they could and dumped the carbonized rejects on the ground. Then all the girls went to bed in sleeping bags with a large plastic groundsheet under them and another on top. They lay side by side in their bags like cordwood, talked till nearly midnight, and finally dropped off to sleep.

For propriety's sake, Jerry Chase had camped alone about fifty feet below the logjam, with Sage tied up not far away on the end of a twenty-eight-foot manny rope, and long after he had heard the last peep out of the girls, the young algebra and history teacher had been unable to find sleep.

This was a new experience for Jerry Chase. On his own, he had camped in the middle of the deepest, wildest forests with no fear whatever. His career included terms as a bareback and bull rider in a traveling rodeo, and all through his life he had hunted big game in the deep wildernesses of the North. Once, a huge grizzly had marched straight down the snowy trail below the place where Chase's feet were dangling from a rock, and neither the grizzly nor the hunter had swerved an inch. Another time, Chase shot a bull elk and left it to cool out overnight, and when he returned at dawn, two grizzlies had reduced the hundreds of pounds of meat to a single forequarter. Chase shooed them off.

But this trip into Glacier Park was different. Now the Chases were not only responsible for themselves, but for the six young girls camped up the trail. If there was a maverick grizzly around, it could descend on that camp and inflict heavy injuries on all the girls before they would even know what was happening, before they could make a move to defend themselves or run away. Lying in his sleeping bag, listening to the lake waters lap at the logjam, Jerry Chase remembered previous grizzly incidents in the great park. He knew that no one had ever been killed by a bear in Glacier—at least no one of record—and he also knew that the last serious injury had been four or five years before. But the laws of probabilities that he taught in his junior-high school math classes were of no consolation here in the wilderness. He remembered all the fresh sign on the trail, the tins with teeth marks in them, the torn jeans, the big pile of debris underneath the spruce tree off the trail.

When there was this much evidence of grizzly activity, the general laws of probability lost their meaning; a whole new set of permutations and combinations took over.

Sometime after midnight, Jerry Chase found himself sitting

straight up in his sleeping bag, wondering if he had been awakened by a real noise or by his overactive imagination. There it was again, a small splash in the water just on the other side of the logjam. He had seen plenty of trout feeding on the surface at night, but this noise did not have the typical *splat* of a rising fish. Chase listened hard, and once again he heard an unnatural movement of water, as though something were pushing through the lake: an oar, or a hoof, or a paw. Sage whinnied loudly and began moving up and down on her long rope, and the splashing sound increased sharply. Chase jumped from his bag, grabbed his flashlight, and ran down to the lakeside. But there was a heavy haze, and he could see nothing. It took him a long time to get back to sleep.

The girls began to stir just after dawn, and young Karen Lyons, at one end of the row, asked Sharon Chase, "Did you get up and go to the bathroom in the woods during the night?"

Mrs. Chase said that she had not.

"Well, somebody did, and they stepped on my foot," the child said.

Sharon Chase asked the girls one by one if they had slipped into the woods during the night, and all but one said no. The single exception was a girl who had been sleeping at the opposite end of the row from Karen Lyons. She had gotten up during the night but had not gone anywhere near Karen. Immediately, the girls concluded that a bear had invaded the camp and stepped on Karen Lyons, and all the cajoling and joking of the elder couple could not kid them out of it. The fact that the charred popcorn had disappeared from the ground did not help to calm matters, and when someone said, "Look, the ground squirrels could have done that," someone else said, "Yeah, and so could the grizzlies."

The day was spent on tenterhooks. Some of the girls went fishing, but Susie Sampson and one of her friends stayed near the camp all day. Once they made a tentative foray out toward the center of the logjam, but they had hardly set foot on the bleached tamarack trunks when they both jumped a foot; a long reddish animal had appeared from a chink in the logs ahead of them, and now it was telling them off in a loud chatter and flashing its bright white teeth. The girls jumped to another log and ran back to the camp, but their excited description of the animal did not add up to anything that Jerry Chase could identify. "Probably an otter," the teacher said, "or maybe a marten, nothing to worry about." The girls were not satisfied with this information, and they steadfastly refused to approach the logjam anymore.

By three o'clock, all the girls were assembled in the camp; there were dozens of minor miracles to be seen in the woods around them and dozens of things to be accomplished by Girl Scouts here in the park, but they did not have the heart for anything except staying around the adults and the fire. It was early for dinner, but the girls held a democratic council and decided that they had no further interest in Trout Lake. They had intended to stay three days, but now they decided to hike out to civilization as soon as they finished the steaks that Jean Gillespie had brought. Perhaps some other time....

After dinner, the girls busied themselves assembling their packs. Pat Sampson, Susie's twin, yanked on a rope that led to the manny bag hanging high in a tree, but the knot stuck and the canvas bag would not come down. Pat was the athletic type, and without being asked, she shimmied straight up the tree and began working on the jammed knot. "OK bear," she shouted from twenty feet up, "I'm ready for you now! "

Somebody on the ground said, "very funny."

When the knot was undone, Pat slid down the tree like a fire fighter, and just as she hit the ground, she lifted a shaking finger and pointed toward the tree where the pony was tied and almost screamed, "There he is! "

Jerry Chase thought that the kidding had gone far enough, and he started to admonish the child when something caught his eye from the direction in which she was pointing. He turned and saw a brownish bear with silvertipped mane, creeping up on the dozing pony. "Yeah," he said in a soft voice, "there he is, and he's a grizzly!"

The bear was almost upon Sage when the gray pony bolted and dashed to the end of its tether toward the lake. The bear reared up and dropped down, in one continuous motion, and took after the pony on all fours. Sage waited till the bear was almost upon her again, and then sidestepped nimbly and ran past the grizzly to the opposite end of her twenty-eight-foot rope. She stood on top of a little bench and pawed the ground and whinnied with terror, but instead of giving chase again, the bear stopped at the pony's saddle blanket, sat down, and began gnawing on it.

"Get up the hill!" Chase shouted, and the six members of Girl Scout Troop 367, accompanied by Sharon Chase, scrambled up the slope behind the trail. When they had gone thirty or forty feet, they stopped and looked. Jerry was running toward his pony, and the bear was dining on the scraps of hashed-brown potatoes left over from dinner. "Never mind the bear!" Sharon Chase said. "Find trees!" But they were in the part of the woods where the trees were either stunted or lacked branches on the lower trunks, and not all the girls could climb straight up like Pat Sampson. So the group stayed together and ran farther up the hillside till they had put about fifty feet between them and the bear, which by now was munching away on everything in sight in the campground. All the packs had been placed in a neat line against the side of a fallen tree, and one by one the bear was opening them. In one, it found an apple and devoured it in a gulp. In another pack, it found a baby-food jar of jelly and chewed and swallowed the whole thing, including the glass.

Jerry Chase came running up the slope below the girls just as the bear turned to an expensive pack that had been borrowed from a doctor in Kalispell. As the bear stuck a claw into the sixty-dollar pack, one of the girls lost her temper and threw a rock at the animal. When the grizzly showed no signs of resentment, the whole group began throwing, but the stones did not seem to have the slightest effect. Jerry Chase picked up a rock almost too heavy to carry, crept to within twenty feet of the bear, and slammed it into the animal's thin ribs. The grizzly woofed once and kept on eating. From her position higher on the hill, Sharon Chase threw smaller stones, and when one of them caught the bear full in the nose, it jumped up and retreated toward the logjam, pawing at its face. After only a few seconds, it dashed off the logs and headed up the hill toward its tormentors.

Jerry Chase grabbed a handful of rocks and told the girls that he would hold off the bear while they circled back to the campsite and salvaged what was left for a hurried trip out. The bear was quartering the brush toward the girls, and the girls were circling away and working down toward the camp. Chase intruded himself in the middle and began pelting the bear with stones. As the girls reached the camp and grabbed what was left, the schoolteacher and the bear reached the main trail that paralleled the lakeshore, alternately chasing each other. The man would hit the bear in a tender spot, and the animal would race up the trail toward Arrow Lake, but as soon as the teacher got close enough for his next salvo, the bear would come woofing down the trail at him. In this yo-yo fashion, man and bear reached a point about 150 yards from the camp, where the lake trail made a slight turn, when all at once the bear seemed to tire of the game and charged at full speed. The brave schoolteacher stood his ground and let fire several rocks, but the grizzly hesitated only slightly, and Chase fled all the way back to the camp. As he did, he saw the bear above him on the trail disappearing toward a thicket by the logjam. "He's gone!" Chase hollered. "Let's get out of here!" He had thrown a saddle on the pony and started tying on the manny bag when his wife shouted, "Here he comes again! "

The grizzly had reappeared on the trail below the logjam.

Sharon said, "I'll try and hold him off while you tie the bag."

With her husband yanking feverishly on the ropes, Sharon Chase walked toward the bear and threw a small rock. The animal stopped and studied the scene of frenzied activity less than fifty feet away and then calmly lay down on the trail. Sharon returned to the group, and the bear continued watching them, resting its head on its forepaws like a puppy. The pony rolled her eyes back in their sockets and pulled against her tether, and Sharon tried to hold the frightened animal by the halter, but the movements were too strong for her. "I can't hold her!" she shouted, and Chase said, "Take the girls and get out! "

The troop ran ahead, followed by the man and the lurching pony, and as soon as the area was cleared of humans, the grizzly pulled itself slowly to its feet and started across the end of the logjam toward the camp. By now, it was plain that the animal was more interested in food scraps than Girl Scouts, and Susie Sampson felt safe enough to pull out her Kodak Instamatic and snap a picture from the crest of the hill that led downtrail to safety.

It was dark, and the group was exhausted when the dirt road around Lake McDonald finally came into view. There was talk about stopping and reporting the affair to the local ranger, but Jerry Chase failed to see the point. "They can read," he said, "and they've seen all those remarks on the trail register by now. We'd just be telling them something they already know."

When the group got back to Kalispell, thirty miles south of Glacier Park, Susie Sampson told her regular scout leader that they had seen a grizzly bear. "Oh, come on," the woman said, and laughed. But then Susie took her roll of film to the *Daily Inter Lake,* Kalispell's only daily newspaper, and on Thursday, August 10, 1967, a picture of the Trout Lake bear appeared on page one.

The next day, a hard-driving newspaperman went to Glacier

Park to peddle his papers and have a few words with some of his friends, the ranger officials. Mel Ruder, holder of a master's degree in sociology, had been reporting, writing, photographing, editing, proofreading, and selling the local news for twenty-two years, and his weekly *Hungry Horse News* had won more plaques and trophies than there was room for in the tiny office in Columbia Falls. Ruder had won the Pulitzer Prize two years earlier for his reporting of a flood that inundated Glacier Park, but the prize changed nothing in his life. He still worked twelve hours a day, Monday through Friday, and then spent weekends taking photographs for the next week's paper with his old-fashioned Speed Graphic camera; he still sold his own advertising, and he still ran around the county every Friday afternoon with fresh-run copies of the *Hungry Horse News* under his arm, planting them in dispensers and giving away as many as he sold.

"They know me up in the park," Ruder said with studied understatement later, "and I love to mind their business for them. I've been around here longer than any of the rangers, and I tell them off, and they like me and I like them. We can speak frankly."

On this day, Ruder told anyone in headquarters who would listen, including the superintendent, that a dangerous situation had developed at Trout Lake. "Just look at the facts," Ruder said as he collared one ranger executive. "This bear's been around all summer. People have written about him. I wrote about him myself the other day when he chased Steve Ashlock and John Cook. And now that bear's not only being written about, but its picture is running in the *Inter Lake!*"

The rangers at headquarters told him that they were busy with fires, but they would see what could be done. Ruder left to peddle his papers elsewhere, but he could not rid himself of the fear that any day now, there would be trouble.

— 5 —

THE LONG WEEKEND

Miss Joan Devereaux, 22 years old and barely out of college, stopped every now and then to call the group's attention to some wonder of nature. The brown-haired ranger-naturalist had majored in botany at Miami University of Ohio and Ohio State, so her trailside lectures tended more toward plant life, just as certain other naturalists tried to stick to geology or zoology or some other subject of easy familiarity. Miss Devereaux hoped that the devoted bird watchers in her group would not rely too heavily on her. She had heard them chattering, and it was plain that four or five of them were walking encyclopedias of ornithology. Joan Devereaux, in her first year as a ranger-naturalist conducting guided tours through the park, felt somewhat shaky when it came to birds. She could get just as excited as the next person over the sight of a snowy owl or a goshawk, but she was frankly no expert, and every time the bird watchers came near, she managed to steer the conversation toward flora. "See this bright yellow flower," she would say in her most charming manner.

"This is a butterwort, and it is an insectivorous plant. Did I get that right? In-sec-ti-vor-ous. That means it eats insects. It's sort of like a pitcher plant. Insects will get trapped in the sticky stuff on the leaves and then the plant produces an acid that kind of devours them. Basically the plant wants the nitrogen in the insect. Butterwort is the name."

When Joan had gone to work that morning, she had learned that she was to make her maiden guided tour of one of the most spectacular trails in the world: the 7.6-mile Highline Trail from Logan Pass to Granite Park Chalet. The young botanist had been on the trail before, but only as a visitor. Her own guided tours were usually shorter, but on this Saturday, August 12, every available male on the Park Service's roster had been rushed into fire-fighting duties; there had been an electrical storm the day before, and fire watchers had spotted more than 100 ground strikes and 21 "smokes." By the next morning, the acrid smell of disaster was in the air. Joan had heard about the hot strikes, and she was not surprised when she was told that Fred Goodsell was on the fire lines and she would have to conduct his overnight tour into Granite Park Chalet.

There were thirty-six hikers plus the girl guide, and they ranged in age from a woman of about 65 to a 9-month-old baby boy, backpacked by his sturdy father. At first, the trail cut into the side of dark, sheer cliffs; a single misstep could send a hiker plunging several hundred feet down, and the group picked its way carefully. But soon the trail reached steeply sloping mountainsides thickly carpeted with fields of berries: There were bunchberries, thimbleberries, huckleberries, twinberries, gooseberries, serviceberries, raspberries, and several other varieties. The whole hillside looked as though it had been designed and planted solely on behalf of the Ursus family, the world's most enthusiastic berriers, but Joan quickly explained to the hikers that they were still fairly close to the

Going-to-the-Sun Highway, a few hundred feet below them, and despite the profusion of berries, grizzly bears had almost never been spotted here in the summer. This brought a sigh of relief from the hikers and the usual round of bear jokes, but Joan did not join in. Every day, she talked to her fellow naturalists, and one of the subjects they discussed most was the blatant feeding at Granite Park Chalet. She was wondering how she would react to it firsthand.

After an hour or two of walking, the group came to a place where the trail snaked a few thousand feet below the jagged top of the Garden Wall, a gigantic razor's edge of sharply banded rock that marked the edge of the Continental Divide. Ages before, a pair of giant glaciers had come scooping their way through the upthrust of an ancient sea and scalloped out the valleys on each side of the cliff. Where the two glaciers had almost come together on their parallel routes, they had carved out a thin slice of wall that towered, serrated and crumbling, high above the hikers. A few hundred feet down from the top, white dots moved slowly about; they were mountain goats, finding something to nibble in an area that looked bare of all life. Now and then, one would frolic in a little mountain-goat two-step and then look wisely down at the tourists below. Somebody in the crowd said that this was typical mountain-goat behavior; so long as they had the upper foot, they acted relaxed and unperturbed.

It was just before noon, and the caravan had been on the trail for nearly three hours, when Joan led the hikers up a sharply contoured switchback and into sight of Granite Park, two miles away on the lava flow. The view was always inspiring to panting hikers, and Joan ordered a lunch break alongside a field of asters. The rest of the hike was uneventful, except that the birdwatchers were excited when a calliope hummingbird, slightly larger than a bee, buzzed into sight, followed quickly by a golden eagle. Joan was no birder, but she shared the thrill at the sight of these two spectacular specimens. By one thirty, the weary party had crossed the last two miles of subalpine terrain, alongside alder and fir trees and an occasional limber pine, and reached the bulky old chalet. On the schedule was a short rest and a hike to the nearby Mount Grinnell overlook, but the day had been fiercely hot, and not one of the young naturalist's charges opted for the pleasure. Mostly they sat around the front porch of the chalet and watched the smokes that signaled distant fires. A few picked flowers, and some went inside the giant mountain hut to form one of those laughing, happy round-table groups that can be found not only in Glacier Park but on the Mont Blanc, the Swiss Alps, the Dolomites, wherever people gather to cast aside their inhibitions and their cares in the special giddiness of altitude. Joan went from group to group, answering questions, trying to be of assistance, and she could not help laughing with the revelers when one of them pointed out the last item on the blackboard menu next to the kitchen. "Grizzly burgers," it read, "all sold out."

As she was standing at the main entrance to the chalet, the girl in the green Park Service uniform was approached by a young couple whom she did not recognize from the tour. They told her that their name was Klein and that they had hiked in alone, and they wondered if she could tell them where the overnight camping area was. Still in the gay mood of the crowd inside, Joan pointed down the hill toward the Granite Park campground and said, "Did you bring your grizzly repellent with you?" When Mrs. Klein seemed concerned, the young naturalist told her that there were some grizzlies around, but that people did indeed camp in the area below the chalet, and they were welcome to do the same. The Kleins thanked her and walked off, talking animatedly to each other.

After dinner, the traditional community sing began, slowly at first, but at last threatening the heavily timbered walls of the building. Right in the middle of "Row, Row, Row Your Boat," a young girl burst into the big dining room and shouted, "They're here! They're here! Here's the big attraction! "

Joan knew what the girl meant, and she hushed the group and announced in a flat voice, "Well, supposedly they're here. The bears, that is. I'm sure you've all heard about them. Now why don't you just go quietly around this way and up to the balcony and watch them from a safe place?" But she had not even finished her suggestion when the crowd, by now swollen to sixty or sixty-five by hikers who had arrived later, began to elbow past her toward the back door. They spilled into the night and milled around at ground level trying to see over one another. About fifty yards away, a small silvertip nibbled at something on the ground.

Joan Devereaux looked briefly at the bear and found herself in instant agreement with the idea she had heard expressed so often by her senior naturalists. She did not profess to be an expert on bears, let alone on the huge grizzlies, but it seemed to her that there was genuine danger in the proximity of murmuring humans and feeding bears. Over and over, she had heard naturalists say that sooner or later something had to happen, and now she could see why. A few of the bolder onlookers crept down the gully to be closer to the feeding animal, and the young lady naturalist turned away from the scene and walked to the front porch of the chalet. For a while, she stared across the valley of McDonald Creek toward Heaven's Peak, 9,000 feet high, and watched the sun sink in shades of purple and pink and crimson and give way suddenly to a crisp slice of moon, vivid and sharp in the early evening. Thin shafts of smoke from a few small fires in the valley stood straight and tall in the moonlight, like columns of pale steel, and there was the faintest smell of burning wood on the air. Joan thought briefly that she had never seen so calm or so beautiful a night, and then the deep fatigue of the long, hard day set in, and she went inside to bed.

The Kleins, Robert and Janet, had not been married long enough for major arguments, but now they were having a major disagreement. Janet had heard about the bears of Granite

Park Chalet, and she announced that there was no force on Earth, including her handsome six-foot seven-inch husband, that could get her to sleep out in the campground that night. For his part, Robert still was not convinced that the presence of a few bears should change their plans for a night underneath the limitless vault of the sky. Janet was more than a foot shorter than her husband and weighed barely 100 pounds, but she stood her ground and finally announced that big brave Robert could sleep outside if he wanted to, but she was going to scrape $12.50 out of her packsack and sleep in the chalet.

"You would do that?" the shocked husband asked.

"I certainly would," said the determined young lady.

It was odd how the subject of bears had come up so often on the young couple's camping trip. Nothing had been further from their minds when they had planned the two-week excursion into Glacier National Park. Robert, a 23-year-old geologist originally from Denver, and Janet, a 23-year-old schoolteacher originally from Nebraska, were both in love with the outdoors, and when they acquired a fancy new Japanese camera and some vacation time simultaneously, they decided to put both to use on a camping trip. The idea might have been sound, but an immediate complication set in: On one of their first day hikes in Glacier Park, they left the camera at their luncheon site, and when they returned to retrieve it, the camera was gone. "That should have tipped us off right away that we were operating under a dark cloud," Janet said later, "but all we did was borrow a camera from a friend and keep right on going."

The friend was Robert Frauson, ranger-in-charge of most of the eastern portion of the park and one of the most highly respected rangers in the Park Service. The Kleins were glad to have a contact in the green ranger uniform when they first arrived from their home in Longmont, Colorado. They had a long talk with Frauson, and they listened interestedly when the subject of grizzlies came up. Frauson told them that there was always the possibility of running into a bear and that they should carry bells or other noisemakers with them, or sing or talk loudly as they walked. If they took these simple precautions, the boss ranger said, it was extremely unlikely that they would even see a grizzly.

"And what if we do?" Janet asked.

"Well, there's no set thing," Frauson said. "You can't outrun them, that's for sure, so maybe the best thing is to run for a tree, and if you can't find a tree, just roll up in a fetal position and take whatever the bear dishes out."

The Kleins had all but forgotten Frauson's advice in the general exuberance and delight of planning a seven-mile hike to Granite Park Chalet a few days later. To be sure, they wore their bear bells as they set out from Logan Pass a few hours after Joan Devereaux's party on Saturday, but as they picked their way along the tall cliffs and gazed across McDonald Valley at the mauve-, purple-, and pink-banded peaks that shattered the skyline, bears were forgotten. Bob Klein clicked his borrowed camera at marmots and ground squirrels and mountain goats and almost anything that moved, including his slender wife, and despite the soaring heat of the day and the sniff of wood fire that tinted the air, their packs had never felt lighter.

They were munching on their lunch at the midway point of the hike when another family pulled up and joined them in the easy informality of the trail. "Are you gonna sleep out?" one of the newcomers asked, seeing the Kleins' packs.

"Sure," Robert Klein answered.

"Where? "

"Oh, we don't know. Somewhere around the chalet, I guess."

The man asked the Kleins if they had heard about the bears, and the couple said that they knew there were grizzlies in Glacier Park, but they had heard nothing specific about Granite Park.

"Well," the newcomer said, "they've got 'em."

Shortly before three in the afternoon, Janet and Robert Klein were taking a break about a quarter mile from their destination when a party of four hikers overtook them—a mother and father and two teenage daughters. Once again, the conversation turned to grizzlies, and once again the Kleins were asked if they intended to sleep out. "It's your own business what you do," the father said, "but I can tell you for sure, there's at least five grizzlies that hang around that chalet, and you wouldn't catch me camping out there for a million dollars."

As they walked slowly on the last leg of their long hike, the Kleins realized that the subject of grizzlies seemed to be on everybody's tongue, but they still did not know how seriously to take the information that was being offered to them in job lots. They walked up to the front door of the lonely mountain blockhouse, eased their packs to the ground, and spotted a pretty brown-haired girl wearing the uniform of the National Park Service. Klein brought up the subject of grizzlies, and the young woman said that she had just conducted her first guided tour into Granite Park, but she had been told by any number of old hands that several bears came into the chalet area each night for handouts.

Still, she said, people camped in the woods below the chalet, and the grizzlies did not seem to disturb them.

Robert Klein was surprised and asked the naturalist if she was kidding. "I wish I were," the naturalist answered, "but I'm not."

The conversation frightened Janet Klein and disturbed her husband more than a little.

"OK," he said, "we'll see about staying in the chalet."

They were told that the young man in charge of the rooms was in the back burning trash, and the Kleins walked around the big log and stone building and introduced themselves to a sturdily built bearded man who told them his name was Tom Walton. By now, it was late afternoon, and Walton said that he was sorry, but every bed was booked. "What about the floor?"

Klein asked, and Walton told them they could sleep on the floor and enjoy three full meals for $25.

"For sleeping on the floor?" Klein asked in amazement

"Well, that's the rate," Walton said pleasantly. "I'd like to make exceptions, but I just can't."

Klein asked if they could lay out their sleeping bags in one of the washrooms that lay huddled about the chalet, but the innkeeper told them that this was against the rules, and if he bent the rules for one couple, he would soon have campers choking up the washrooms and sleeping alongside the toilets, and no one would be satisfied with that arrangement.

"Well, OK," Robert Klein said, "then tell us frankly, what's the bear situation around here? That seems to be all anybody talks about."

Walton told them that two grizzlies had been coming in on a regular basis for two or three weeks now, that they came from the trail that led down toward the trail cabin and the campground and returned by the same route, and that they did not appear to represent an immediate danger to anyone. "They come in, eat their scraps, and leave, and that's that," Walton said.

"And they head down toward the campground?" Klein asked.

"In that general direction," Walton said. "But I wouldn't worry about it. Hundreds of people have camped there this summer, and the bears haven't eaten anybody yet." The two men laughed, but Janet Klein gulped and told herself that the campground was out so far as she was concerned. Walton went about his chores, and the young couple discussed their problem. At first they had been in total agreement that it would be ridiculous to pay $25 to sleep on the floor of the chalet. But now Janet was thoroughly frightened, and she delivered her ultimatum that she would find the money and stay inside in safety. Robert said he wanted to think about it some more and left for a quick climb up to Swiftcurrent Lookout, 1,000 feet above.

When he returned, it was about six thirty, and Janet introduced him to a 20-year-old hiker from Paradise, California, named Don Gullett. Janet had noticed Gullett's pack and his sleeping bag and had asked him how he could entertain the idea of sleeping out in this grizzly-infested area. Gullett had told her that he was not worried about the bears, and he had staked out a nice flat spot in the shadow of the trail cabin. Robert Klein asked Gullett how far it was from the trail cabin to the campground. "Oh, several hundred yards anyway," Gullett answered, and the three agreed to walk down the trail along the lava flow and take a look.

By now, Janet Klein was wondering if she was not overreacting and threatening her husband's enjoyment unreasonably. The trail cabin site was charming; a tiny stream tinkled alongside, and there were big patches of purple asters and red monkey flower and cinquefoil. Off to the southwest, one could make out the general area of the campground, but it seemed a safe distance away. The logs at the edges of the trail cabin had been laid out in an overlapping crisscross pattern, providing four natural ladders to the galvanized metal roof, and when Robert pointed out that they could get up the side in seconds if a grizzly came around, Janet announced bravely that the site met her approval. The Kleins made camp just below the lava flow, some 20 feet from the uphill wall of the cabin, and Gullett laid his bag alongside the lower wall.

"Now let's forget about bears and enjoy ourselves," Robert Klein said, and the young couple began preparing supper while Gullett busied himself about 30 feet away. The Kleins were preparing to eat when a pair of teenagers arrived and asked where the campground was. When Robert Klein pointed off to the left, the boy, who called himself Roy and looked to be about 18, said, "Well, if the campground's over there, why are the three of you camping here?"

"If you want to know the truth," Janet Klein said, "we're afraid of bears."

The Granite Park Chalet, where tourists to Glacier National Park gathered nightly during two months of the year to watch resident grizzlies feed on garbage, is about 500 yards above the campsite where Julie Helgeson was killed.

Thirteen-year-old Girl Scout Susie Sampson took this picture of a grizzly at Trout Lake just a few days before the bear killed Michele Koons at a campsite near here.

During the six weeks before the attacks, several residents and visitors lodged concerns with Park Service personnel about a bear behaving strangely and without fear of humans at Trout Lake and nearby Kelly's Camp, but rangers did nothing about it.

Top, left, *Michele Koons, a 19-year-old from San Diego California, was working for the summer in the gift shop at Lake McDonald Lodge when she was violently killed by a grizzly bear during an overnight camping trip near Trout Lake.* Bottom, left, *Julie Helgeson, 19, a sophomore at the University of Minnesota, had been in Glacier Park for two months, working in the laundry at East Glacier Lodge, when she took her first overnight hike. She headed into the wilderness near Granite Park Chalet, where she was killed by a different grizzly on the same night, miles away from Koons.*

Facing page, top, *Dr. Olgierd Lindan (head bent), a visitor to the Granite Park Chalet on the night of the grizzly attacks, helped attend to the victims. Here, Lindan and others grieve about the tragedies on the day after.* Facing page, bottom, *22-year-old ranger-naturalist Joan Devereaux completed her maiden guided tour of the 7.6-mile Highline Trail from Logan Pass to Granite Park Chalet with 36 hikers on August 12. When tragedy struck that night, she found herself thrust in the position of commanding the rescue.*

Above, *the site where Roy Ducat and Julie Helgeson were camping when they were attacked. This site is some nine crow miles and on the other side of the 9,000-foot cliffs and spires of the Livingstone Range from where Michele Koons was killed by another grizzly on that same night.* Left, *rescuers used Roy Ducat's sleeping bag and a set of bedsprings that had been nailed across the outside of one of the windows at the trail cabin to keep out bears to fashion a stretcher to carry Ducat back to the Granite Park Chalet.*

Facing page, top, *is a view—looking northeast—of the area where Julie Helgeson was attacked in the Granite Park Campground. The bear dragged the victim downhill (toward the camera).* Facing page, bottom, *campers Janet and Robert Klein and hiker Don Gullet were camped next to this trail cabin when Ducat and Helgeson were attacked at the Granite Park Campground, some 100 yards or so away. The badly injured Ducat made it to this site to get help after the attack.*

*Rangers and volunteers dragged the dead female bear be-
lieved to have killed Julie Helgeson from the Granite Park
Chalet to a helicopter landing site. "Bear No. 3", the third
one killed in the aftermath, was shot 48 hours after the
deadly attack.*

When Park Service bi-
ologist Cliff Martinka,
right, examined the
claw of the dead female
grizzly two days after
the killings, he said,
"We got her. This is the
one."

In examining the bear's
paw, below, Martinka
found traces of dried
blood matted in the
hairy spaces between
claws, as well as an old
injury that the biologist
believed would have
kept the bear in constant
pain—and in an angry
mood.

Above, *hiker Don Gullet with the bear believed to have killed Julie Helgeson. The grizzly weighed about 260 pounds and had two cubs.* Below, *on the day after it was killed, Bear No. 3 was stuffed into a helicopter and returned to park headquarters for examination.*

Rangers gathered around the carcass of Bear No. 3, as seen from the balcony of the Granite Park Chalet, where rangers were standing when they shot the bear. This photo shows the distance from the Chalet to the garbage feeding area; on the left is the trail to the campground where Helgeson was killed.

Park Service seasonal ranger-biologist Dave Shea and hiker Don Gullet stand over the scene where Julie Helgeson was attacked, with the Granite Park Chalet a quarter mile southeast of the men in the background.

The younger couple laughed. "Oh, that's nothing to worry about," the boy said, and his companion, an attractive girl of about the same age, laughed again as though the subject were a joke. The teenage boy proceeded to tell a humorous story about grizzly bears, but later on no one was able to remember it. The girl, Julie, flashed a beautiful smile and said, "Well, let's get going," and the young couple bounced away toward the campground. The Kleins finished their dinner and carried all their refuse up to the chalet trash cans, hung around to talk, and returned by way of the upper edge of the lava flow, the better to watch the spectacular sunset. Then they covered their provisions with plastic and hauled them to the top of a medium-sized subalpine fir and climbed into their sleeping bag. "Now tell me again," Janet said, as the two of them lay under the bright moon and stars and tried to get to sleep, "what do we do if a bear comes?"

Robert Klein had carefully placed the flashlight and their boots within arm's reach. "We grab these," he said, "and we go up the side of the cabin to the roof." Not long after, the Kleins heard Don Gullett come back down the trail and prepare to turn in, and by ten or ten thirty, they were all asleep.

The campground would never be confused with the Ritz, but to the two young hikers, their heads already filled with the wonder and joy of the wilderness, it was luxurious. The place was in obvious disrepair; the sign—"GRANITE PARK CAMPGR0UND"—lay on the earth, as did beams and metal braces and other building materials, but at least there was a fire pit, and someone had left a few logs for the next campers. The boy and the girl looked at each other and smiled and nodded and headed back to the chalet to pick up the packs that they had left behind while they reconnoitered the area.

Except for the fact that they were an exceedingly handsome young couple, there was little to distinguish Roy Ducat and Julie Helgeson from the 850 other students who worked for park concessioners as waiters and busboys and cooks and clerks and

valets and on other assignments befitting their tender years and
their willingness to work cheaply. If all these young people had
one characteristic in common, it was the brashness of youth.
Early each summer, the park rangers would give lectures about
the park and its dangers, and attendance was compulsory
for the young employees, but none of them seemed to learn
much from the lectures—or so the older rangers grumbled. It
was a fact that the death and accident rates were high among
the youngsters. Nobody kept score, but Mel Ruder, the newspaperman who kept a studious eye on the park from a range
of fifteen miles away, once estimated that an average of one
employee per year did not return home alive. They died on
mountain climbs for which they were not prepared, on narrow
roads they refused to respect, and in high-altitude lakes that
were twenty degrees colder than the lakes back home. "But
thank God none of them ever died at the hands of grizzlies,"
Ruder said, "and maybe this is why the kids would yawn and
hold hands and close their ears when the rangers would tell
them about the danger from bears. The kids would sort of say
to themselves, 'What danger? Name me one kid that's been
killed and I'll listen to you.'"

Dorothy Love, manager of the gift shop at Lake McDonald
Lodge, put it another way. "These kids come in from everywhere. Some of them do know something about the outdoors—
but only where they came from. They may be Pennsylvania
knowledgeable, and they might be Tucson knowledgeable, but
they aren't Montana knowledgeable."

Roy Ducat, working for the summer as a busboy at East
Glacier Lodge, was Ohio knowledgeable and a cut above most
of his young colleagues, both intellectually and physically. At
18, he was already a sophomore in biology at Bowling Green
State University, not far from his home in Perrysburg, Ohio.
He was not overpoweringly strong, but he could hold his own
on an all-day hike; he had worked as a lifeguard, and he kept
himself in shape.

His companion, Julie Helgeson, was Minnesota knowledge-able, a lovely slender girl with brown hair and blue eyes and a deep interest in nature. At 19, she was already two years out of high school, where she had been a pompon girl, a singer in the school choir, and a class leader. Now a sophomore at the University of Minnesota, she kept up her active life in the church. Her father liked to describe her in a short phrase—"a beautiful, bubbling girl."

Julie had been in Glacier Park for two months, working in the laundry at East Glacier Lodge, before she felt ready for her first overnight hike into the wilderness. A few days earlier, she had said good-bye to her parents, who had headed back to Albert Lea, Minnesota, after a two-day visit in the park.

Now Julie had met a personable young man named Roy Ducat, and he was to be her companion on the trip to Granite Park Chalet. The two youngsters had filled their packs with camping gear and goodies, picked up sack lunches from the kitchen of the lodge, and hitchhiked the twenty miles to Logan Pass, jumping off point for the eight-mile Highline hike to Granite Park. It was 7 p.m. when they arrived at the chalet and talked to Gullett and the Kleins, and 8 p.m. before they had looked around and finally settled on the official campground for their headquarters. Back at the chalet, getting their packs, they noticed table scraps behind the back wall, but Roy had already heard about the bears that visited the place, and he was not especially worried. They would be sleeping 500 yards away. Just before they started down the trail for the night, a woman asked them where they were headed. "To the camp-ground," Roy said.

"But that's exactly where the bears come from," the woman said. "Aren't you afraid? "

The two young people laughed and said they were not afraid.

They laid out their sleeping bags, nibbled at their sack lunches and enjoyed the sunset, and just before dark, Roy remembered something he had heard about bears. He carried the dinner leftovers to a log about 200 yards away and cached them underneath. The chill of nighttime was descending on the campground, and the youngsters decided to sleep in their clothes, except for their hiking boots. Roy wore blue denim pants and a short-sleeved shirt, and Julie wore cutoff jeans and a blouse. Snuggled into their soft sleeping bags, they were warm and contented, and they chatted for a while as the last slivers of daylight faded down the mountain. Then they were asleep. Sometime later, Roy was awakened by a rustling noise; he sat up and saw a squirrel working the night shift. The boy tiptoed to the nearby brook for a drink of water and then went back to sleep.

∞

The bear's agility amazed Dr. Lindan. "It moved with terrific speed and grace," he told friends later. "So smooth! At the zoo, you have the impression that they are sluggish and slow, but the speed of that bear as it moved up and down was absolutely amazing. After it had fed, it ran like a kitten into the trees, and I remember saying to myself, 'My God, there is no way to escape a beast like that.' It was remarkable."

In his own way, Dr. Olgierd Lindan, associate professor of medicine at Western Reserve University in Cleveland, was as remarkable as the bears. Born in Riga, Latvia, he had lived in Russia and Poland and England, worked as a doctor in Africa, crossed the Sahara, and once walked from southeast France across Andorra and Spain and into Portugal, fleeing the Nazis. As a result of all his meanderings, he spoke English in a jumbled accent that totally confused the amateur etymologists who tried to pin down his origin, and at least three times a day, the patient, middle-aged internist would have to explain that, yes, he had been born in Latvia, but, no, he had not learned to speak Latvian very well, and, yes, he had once considered Polish as his first language, but then he had gone to school in England, and of course there were the years learning to speak French and Russian and German, and, well, he was really sort of a language potpourri. No sooner would the explanation be finished than someone would come up and say, "By the way, Doctor, where you from?" Olgierd Lindan was used to this, and it troubled him not at all. He was a man for all seasons and all people and all countries. Now his wife had gone to visit relatives in England for the summer, and Dr. Lindan and his teenage son, Nicholas, were hiking in Glacier National Park while she was gone. They had taken many of the trail hikes, and then someone had told them about the bears at Granite Park Chalet, and they were not sorry that they had made the long walk into the chalet to see for themselves. True, they had not been able to distinguish the bear very clearly in the dusk, but then how many people had ever laid eyes on grizzlies in their wild state, clearly or otherwise? Dr. Lindan and his son, Nicholas, returned to the chalet dining room more than satisfied with their experience.

After a while, the other onlookers assembled in the dining room, where the sleeping bags of supernumerary guests already were being unfolded, and a minor argument broke out. Dr. Lindan and his son sat and listened, amused, but did not take part. A middle-aged man had asked for a bottle of beer, and a young employee of the chalet had explained that they did not serve beer. The only liquid refreshment was coffee and lime Kool-aid, neither one of which required hauling bottles or cans up and down the long trail to civilization.

"Look," the man said, "I want a beer. I know you've got some here. Don't worry. I'll pay for it."

The girl explained again that there was no beer, and the man flew into a rage. "Listen, damn it, I want a beer!" he shouted. "I'm ready to pay, so bring it!" The girl reddened and disappeared into the kitchen, and when she did not return, the man and his female companion, also of middle years, grumbled some more and disappeared up the steps. "Oh, my," Dr.

Lindan whispered to Nicholas, "I'm afraid they're heading for our room."

A few minutes later, father and son went to their assigned room and learned that their worst fears had been realized. The room slept five, and two of the five were the annoyed couple. The man was still mumbling to himself, "Jesus Christ, Jesus Christ, a man can't even get a beer!" The woman slid under the covers and within seconds was emitting snores that set the walls to rumbling. "I have heard snoring," Dr. Lindan said later, "but this was *snoring!* Exceptional snoring. *World-class* snoring. And she kept it up."

The Lindans, *pere et fils,* slept fitfully.

In the cast of characters assembled at Granite Park Chalet on the night of Saturday, August 12, there were two men who kept more or less to themselves and did not join in the community singing or the gawking at the bear show or the general chumminess of the chalet. The Reverend Thomas Connolly, SJ, and his friend, Steve Pierre, a full-blooded Kalispel Indian, had been on the trail all day long, and now they were tired. They figured they would have a bite to eat, sleep on the floor of the dining room, and resume their hike at dawn on Sunday.

Like so many Jesuits, Tom Connolly spent far more time out in the open working with people than he did in the faintly scented confessionals and sacristies of the formal church. At 38, he had been working for several years with the impoverished Indians of the Northwest, and there were monuments to his energy throughout the region. One of them was the Indian community center in Spokane, where Steve Pierre worked as a counselor. The two men had become fast friends, and after a certain number of eighty-hour weeks in a row, the priest and the Indian liked to hike as far as their legs would carry them into the wilderness, there to replenish themselves for another sequence of eighty-hour weeks. On such trips, Father Connolly would wear a beat-up old jacket issued by Gonzaga

University, where he was based, and few would ever know he was a priest.

The two men were sitting in the dining room of the chalet, listening to the community sing, and eating sandwiches that were prepared by the kitchen staff for those who arrived after the dinner hour, when someone shouted that the bears had arrived. The priest and the Indian were famished, and they continued to eat while the room suddenly emptied, and it was not until they had finished their meal that they wandered outside to see what was going on. Two men were standing on the balcony, focusing flashlights across the gully, and there in the splotches of white light, a big grizzly bear was feeding. "Those crazy white people!" Steve Pierre said angrily. "They don't know anything about bears! They don't know what they're doing!" To Father Connolly, there was something vaguely obscene about the grizzly display, and he followed his disgusted Indian friend back into the chalet. Mattresses had been laid out in a front lobby, and the two good companions pulled their heads into their sleeping bags and called it a night. Not long afterward, the last lantern was snuffed out, and the blockhouse chalet was asleep.

Earlier on that same broiling Saturday, August 12, a party of youngsters had pushed up and over Howe Ridge with the easy stride of youth. Only the puppy, Squirt, a mixed breed with oversized feet that suggested a trace of German shepherd, had tired once or twice, and when he did, one of the strong young people would carry him like a baby until he had recovered his breath. They were all in a hurry; they had gotten off to a late start, and they wanted to reach Trout Lake in time for some fishing and a relaxed outdoor meal.

There were five in the party, all of them employees of concessioners and all but one of them veteran campers in the backcountry of Glacier National Park. The exception was a 16-year-old boy, Paul Dunn, who had arrived in the park three weeks earlier on a visit with his parents and promptly accepted a summertime job as busboy in the East Glacier Lodge. The season had only a little more than a month to run, and Paul's parents, Barbara and Donald Dunn, had headed back to Edina, Minnesota, and told Paul they would see him after Labor Day. When the boy was asked if he would like to accompany two couples on a weekend campout near a place called Trout Lake, he accepted happily. He had heard nothing in particular about grizzly bears around Trout Lake; indeed, he had barely heard of the lake itself, since he was stationed on the opposite side of the park, across the Divide. But bears did not occupy much of the attention of any teenagers in the park, and Paul Dunn was no exception. Before his parents had gone home, the boy and his family had listened to an orientation lecture by a park ranger, and about all Paul remembered from the talk was the information that a grizzly will not attack you if you do not attack it, and if you see one, just climb a tree. Oh, yes, there was one other point that the ranger had made: "Never take a dog on a trail." The ranger had said something about a poodle or some kind of dog being mangled by a bear the year before, dogs and bears being natural enemies.

Now Paul and the two young couples were cresting Howe Ridge and starting on the trail down toward Trout Lake, and assuredly there *was* a dog with them, but Paul Dunn was not particularly worried. The other four hikers were old hands, and their simple explanation about the dog seemed to make sense: It was true, they had said, that you could not take a willy-nilly stroll through the park with your dog, but it *was* permissible to walk a dog on a leash so long as it remained under human control. Paul did not know that they were wrong, that dogs were not allowed on park trails under any conditions. But the flop-footed Squirt was under human control, and no one in the party considered him a danger. Red-haired Denise Huckle, a 20-year-old summertime room clerk and wintertime college student, had befriended the sick and weakened puppy after it had been abandoned in the park, and before setting out on the hike, she had looked high and low at Lake McDonald Lodge for a leash, finally settling for a strong cord. Now the young animal alternately strained at the cord and begged for attention, and the hikers took turns obliging.

Besides Paul, there were two other young men in the party: the brothers Ray and Ron Noseck of Oracle, Arizona. Ron was 21, a waiter at East Glacier Lodge and Denise's date for the overnight trip. Ray was 23, a service station manager near Lake McDonald Lodge and the other girl's date. Both of the Nosecks were attending dental school at the University of Louisville.

The other girl was Michele Koons, 19, a frail and beautiful young lady who came from San Diego, California, and was about to begin her second year at California Western University. She was working for the summer in the gift shop at Lake McDonald Lodge, where the manager of the shop described her as "a blessing, a girl with a zest for life." Michele's zest for life had taken her to Trout Lake several times before, and unlike Paul Dunn, she was aware that grizzlies frequented the area.

But bears were far from the thoughts of the five park employees as they moved lightly along the downhill switchbacks that led through the heavy forest to the berry bushes on the slopes above the lake. Denise was proud of her dog; although he was still a semiconvalescent and had required occasional assistance on the four-mile hike, Squirt had not uttered a single bark, and everyone agreed that the pleasant puppy was a welcome addition to the group. If there was anything to complain about, it was simply that the day was hot, like all the days of that particular August. Less than twenty-four hours earlier, dry lightning had flashed out of the sky and started fires in the crackling brush, and the slightest trace of pine and spruce and fir smoke hung in the air along the trail. But the hikers were as unconcerned about fire as they were about bears. No one had ever burned to death alongside a mountain lake.

It was just before five in the afternoon when the hikers

reached the broad patches of berry bushes and looked down on the blue-green waters below. The sun slanted into their eyes from its perch atop Rogers Peak, 7,000 feet high on the west side of the lake, and grasshoppers squirted about in the parched dryness, but the slightest trace of a breeze from the lake promised a cool evening. As they neared the logjam camp where they intended to spend the night, the hikers could see circles dappling the water; the cutthroat trout were already feeding on their evening diet of flies, and it would not be long before the skillet would be popping and crackling and the fragrant aroma of frying trout would fill the air. Not even the somber message of a couple of other fishermen could dampen the enthusiasm of the party of five. The fishermen announced that they had been treed for two hours the day before by a very aggressive grizzly. The information was neither unexpected nor particularly frightening to five hikers; getting run up a tree by a bear was part of the adventure and the fun of Glacier Park; they knew that no one had ever been killed, and they doubted that anyone ever would be. As Paul Dunn told his parents back in Minnesota much later, "If there was one thing that was drummed into us, it was that bears wouldn't bother us if we didn't bother them. And we certainly weren't gonna bother them!"

Setting up camp alongside the logjam took a matter of minutes. The hikers were so eager to catch their dinner before nightfall that they did little more than drop their packs and head for the lake, stopping only to cram their food into a single bag and haul it high into a tree. The puppy seemed to sense that an adventure was afoot, and he ran about the feet of the hikers, wagging his tail and asking with his eyes to be included. But he wound up in the arms of Michele Koons, who elected to stay behind in the camp while the others were gone. Michele could watch the dog and tidy up the camp, and when the others returned with their catches, they could get right down to dinner with a minimum of delay. The girl and the dog stayed together for two or three hours, then the others began to return. Paul Dunn had a single cutthroat trout, and he began to prepare it. Michele gave him a supplementary hot dog, and the 16-year-old boy laid both the fish and the frankfurter on top of the fire grate. Soon they were sizzling, and a thin wisp of aromatic smoke followed the gentle off-lake breeze and curled up the hill toward the berry patch. Michele, weary from her preparations for the dinner, was sitting at the edge of the campsite on a stump when she looked into the darkening woods in the direction of the smoke and saw a large shadowy form about ten feet away. She jumped up and said, "Here comes a bear!" Ron Noseck untied the dog's leash, grabbed Squirt in his arms, and joined the others in a headlong flight up the rocky lakeshore away from the logs and campsite. All five of the campers came to a stop about fifty yards away, and they watched as a scrawny grizzly of a brownish hue descended upon their campsite and went to work. The food was lying within easy reach, and the bear strolled from dish to dish, taking big gulps, salivating generously, and licking its chops with a long tongue. Inexplicably, the lean animal grabbed a pack in its mouth and ran a few yards up the hillside with it, but just when the evicted campers were hoping that the grizzly was gone for good, it returned to the camp as suddenly as it had left and resumed eating. When fifteen or twenty minutes had passed and darkness was coming on, someone suggested that they abandon the old camp and spend the night where they were. Denise cradled Squirt in her arms while the other four gathered wood for a new fire. When the fire was ignited, the campers saw the grizzly saunter off in the opposite direction and disappear over the logjam.

Now they hurriedly discussed the situation. Someone suggested that they dash over Howe Ridge to the safety of the Lake McDonald ranger station, but it was already dark, and among them they had only one undersized flashlight. Anyway, the bear had disappeared in the general direction of the trail, and the group decided to stay as far as possible from the peculiar animal. Someone else suggested a flight in the opposite direction, along the lake trail to the Arrow Lake shelter cabin, but then it was remembered that the cabin was jammed full of weekenders, and a two-mile hike to Arrow Lake would force the refugees to depend on the inadequate flashlight to illuminate a trail through some of the thickest brush in the park.

After the bear had been gone for several minutes, the group regained some of its courage and aplomb and fell back, once again, on the notion that nothing would happen so long as they gave the bear a wide berth. Paul and the Nosecks went down the lake to gather up the sleeping bags and a sack of cookies and a package of Cheezits that were left over and returned within a few minutes to the new camp at the water's edge. As a double deterrent to the bear, the campers decided to keep the fire roaring all night and erect a kind of log barrier between them and the old campsite. When a stack of wood had been positioned, the five nervous hikers arranged their sleeping bags in a semicircle around the fire and turned in. Denise looped Squirt's leash over a log next to the fire and patted the dog into place between herself and the log. While the two couples and the young boy from Minnesota whispered away in the general direction of sleep, the girl from Arizona kept a gentle hold on her pet. It was a comfort to both of them. Now and then, one of the men would get up and throw a log on the fire, and soon the little camp was still.

∞

Lying in his uncomfortable bed in Granite Park Chalet, on the other side of a 9,000-foot wall of rock from the campers at Trout Lake, Dr. John Lipinski laughed to himself as he thought about the situation. Thirteen years before, he and his wife, Ann, had grown tired of the industrial dirt and noisy traffic and increasing congestion in the city of Chicago and decided to head for the Wild West, where they could indulge their love of nature and spend day after day hiking on wilderness trails. Lipinski was a surgeon, and his wife was a nurse, and when they had set up practice in the lumber town of Kalispell, Montana, the demands on their skills had been so incessant that it had taken them four years to find the time to make their first overnight hike—into Sperry Chalet, to see the mountain goats. Now, eight years after that momentous occasion, they were on their second overnight hike, into Granite Park to see the bears. With them were their daughter, Terese, 16, and their two adopted sons, Robin, 5, and Karl, 4. They had seen one bear, but not very clearly, and just before they had turned in, Terese had told her parents about a conversation with one of the chalet employees.

"How do the bears get there?" Terese had asked.

"Oh, they come to eat the garbage that we put out," the other young girl replied.

"But don't you think that's kind of dangerous?"

"Well, to tell you the truth, the people come up here to see grizzlies, and we have to show them some. That's what most of them are here for."

Lying in bed half asleep, Dr. Lipinski pondered this explanation and, in truth, he could not find it unreasonable. Years before, he had hitchhiked into Yellowstone and observed the grizzlies being fed, and one night he had heard shots as rangers exterminated a few bears that had lost their fear of man. The surgeon had great respect for park rangers, and he knew that any bear that strayed out of line would be exterminated. The simple fact that the Granite Park bears were still alive was proof enough to Dr. Lipinski that they were harmless.

Fighting insomnia alongside her tall husband, Ann Lipinski was not so relaxed about the matter. She had been brought up in a teeming Polish section of Chicago, unlike her North Dakota-bred husband, and the wilderness still seemed mysterious to her. One could talk to Ann Lipinski for hours about the gentle, shy ways of the big grizzlies, but she would never change her attitude that anything that weighed up to 1,000 pounds and had teeth like tenpenny nails and claws as long and as sharp as switchblade knives was just plain dangerous, always was, always would be.

The night was cool outside, but the thick timbers of the chalet had taken an all-day baking from the sun, and Ann Lipinski pitched and tossed and perspired and worried in the closeness of the overheated room. Her daughter, Terese, lay sleeping, fully dressed, on top of another cot, and the two little boys were dead to the world, and now and then Ann would hear a brief snore from her surgeon-husband, but her own mind raced around and around, and sleep would not come.

She had just decided to get up, put on her clothes, and lie atop the bed like Terese when she heard a tiny noise from the direction of a candy package her husband had left out on the dresser. In the pitch blackness, Mrs. Lipinski could see nothing, but it did not take her long to realize that she was in the presence of a terror almost as menacing as a grizzly—a mouse. She sat horror-stricken, and the noise stopped, and just then her husband jumped up and said, "There's a spider on my nose."

"Oh, John, no!" the woman said. "It's a mouse! Let's get out of here!"

A porch adjoined the upstairs room, and Dr. and Mrs. Lipinski opened the door and went outside, the one to breathe the cool fresh air and the other to escape from the mouse. To calm his nervous wife, the surgeon put the candy package in the wastebasket and removed the wastebasket to the porch. "Now if that dangerous mouse comes around again, he'll stay outside," the doctor told his wife, and the two returned to bed.

But only a few minutes had passed when Mrs. Lipinski felt something nibble at her toe—or thought she did. "John," she said. "John! Something's biting my toe! "

"Don't worry," the sleepy husband said. "It's probably only a mouse."

Ann Lipinski, RN, moved to the edge of the bed and decided

that she would stop trying to sleep and just sit and worry for a while. When she had worried extensively about the mouse, she looked around for other worries and found one in the open door. The night was shudderingly still and thick, and the black hole of the doorway overlooked the gully where the bear had been seen earlier. Mrs. Lipinski thought how simple it would be for one of the big grizzlies to sneak up the stairs and devour her, her two boys, her daughter, and her husband. "Now let's see," the troubled woman said to herself, "what would I do if a grizzly attacked?" She figured she would hustle her family out the door and up on the roof. But what if the bear blocked the door? Mrs. Lipinski got up and checked the window and found it was unlocked. She decided that she would wake her husband, and they would push the children out the window to the safety of the roof the instant the bear appeared. Having settled all this in her mind, Mrs. Lipinski somehow found herself back on the bed, her thoughts becoming more and more indistinct, blessed sleep on its way at last, and just then she heard a muffled scream. It seemed to come from the direction of one of the outside bathrooms, and it occurred to the nurse that someone was being attacked. She shook her husband.

"John!" she said. "There's a lady in trouble. John, did you hear the lady scream? "

Dr. Lipinski raised up from his mattress and said, "Why would a lady be screaming up here?"

"Well, I think she's in the bathroom outside, and somebody's bothering her."

Dr. Lipinski eased himself back on the mattress. "Ann," he said sleepily, "a lady wouldn't be screaming out here."

Mrs. Lipinski slapped her hand to her forehead and said to herself that she had known better times: She itched all over from perspiration, a mouse had been nibbling at her toe, and now her husband was telling her that she was hallucinating. And yet she was convinced that she had heard a human scream and that she had not been dreaming. Now, how was she to convince anybody? Just then, she heard the same sound from the same direction.

"John!" she cried. "A lady screamed! I tell you, she's in trouble!"

Dr. Lipinski had fallen back into a half sleep, and once again he suggested that his wife was imagining things or dreaming. "Now, why in the world would a lady be screaming way up here?" he said thickly, and rolled over.

"Somebody's bothering her, John!" Mrs. Lipinski said. "There's a fellow bothering her in the bathroom."

"Oh, Ann, a man wouldn't bother a woman up here. The people just aren't like that around here."

Outside, the wall of silence fell again; not a whisper of wind disturbed the night, and Ann Lipinski let her head fall back on the mattress. She was absolutely certain that she had heard a female scream, if not the first time, then certainly the second, but for the life of her she could not figure out how to communicate the fact to her husband. She was pondering the problem when an unmistakable, distinct scream shattered the night, and both of the Lipinskis were on their feet instantly and rushing out to the balcony. As they did, they heard a far-off woman's voice cry, "Get out! Get out! Get away from me!" The doctor and the nurse reached the railing of the balcony and tried to see into the dark night and pinpoint the sound, and then the voice came clear and terrible across the stillness from the slope below. "God help me, he's stabbing me!" There were a few seconds of silence and then, "God help me! Somebody help me! "

Terese was the only member of the Lipinski family who was dressed, and her parents sent her downstairs to awaken the management. Now they knew beyond any question that something was wrong. Ann Lipinski thought she had it figured out, and she told her husband. "My Lord, we've got a murder on our hands. The poor girl must have been out walking and trying to get back to the chalet, and she must have been attacked by some fellow." Her husband peered into the darkness, trying to get a fix on something, on anything, and did not disagree.

Downstairs, Terese was having difficulty awakening the worn-out hikers and finding the leaders. She picked her way among the bodies lying on the floor of the big front room and said softly, "Hello," but all she got in return were a few guttural complaints and some requests to shut up and let decent people sleep. Finally she called out, in teenager fashion, "Hey, who's the head of all this stuff?"

A voice said, "What's the matter?"

"There's a girl in trouble out there," Terese said, and another voice commented from the floor, "Oh, the poor thing!"

When it appeared that the subject was closed, Terese banged loudly on the first door she could find, and in a few seconds a young woman appeared and asked what was the problem. Terese recognized Joan Devereaux, the naturalist who had guided them into the place, and she blurted out that someone was screaming and could be heard from the balcony above. The ranger said gently, "You've been dreaming. Nobody's cried out. Now just go back to bed."

But Terese insisted, and several minutes went by before she was able to convince the drowsy naturalist that something was amiss. Wearily, Joan agreed to go upstairs with the young girl to see what she could hear. When one of the kitchen workers came into the room to find out what was happening, the naturalist told her to get the chalet's shortwave radio and turn it on, just in case. Then she finished lacing her boots, turned to Terese, and said, "Let's go."

∞

Innkeeper Tom Walton and his wife, Nancy, were sound asleep in their upstairs room, No. 3, when a loud banging on their door awoke them both. Tom looked at his watch; it was twelve forty-five, and hastily yanking on a pair of old Levis, he opened the door and saw Helen "Gracie" Lundgren, one of the more levelheaded employees of the chalet. "What's up?" he said.

Gracie Lundgren was plainly frightened, and the words poured out of her. "Tom, oh, Tom!" she said. "The people are all standing out on the balcony, and they say they heard somebody screaming, somebody being murdered out there! "

"Calm down, Gracie!" Walton said. "They didn't hear anybody yelling down there. Nobody yelled, because there's nobody to yell. Now go on back to bed, and tell the others to get back to bed, too!"

He shut the door and took off his Levis and plopped back into bed, but again there was a pounding on the door. "Tom!" the Lundgren girl cried. "They insist! They heard noises!"

Walton tugged his way into his Levis once again and walked out to the balcony. He recognized Joan Devereaux and the Lipinski family and a few others standing quietly, as though they were trying to hear something, but this was one of those typical Granite Park nights when the silence pressed down on the place like a giant bowl of mushroom soup. Tom knew that the total absence of sound was unknown to most people, and he suspected that someone had let his imagination go wild. "There can't be anything wrong out there," he said. "Just listen to how quiet it is."

"I heard screams, and so did my husband," Mrs. Lipinski said.

"From what direction?" Walton asked.

"Straight down," Dr. Lipinski said. "What's down there?"

"A campground."

"Well, somebody's in trouble down there."

Tom Walton still did not agree, but when Dr. Lipinski suggested that someone holler in the direction of the noises and ask if everything was in order, the young innkeeper said he could see no harm in that; everyone in the chalet was awake by now anyway. Dr. Lipinski cupped his hands and shouted, "Is everything OK?"

From a point to the right of the campground, and more from the direction of the trail cabin, a barely discernible male voice floated back on the still night air. "No!" the voice answered.

"What's the trouble? "

The voice answered, "Bear!"

∞

Janet Klein did not know how long the animals had been fighting before she awoke, but now she sat straight in her sleeping bag behind the trail cabin and listened to the shrieks rend the still night. She tried and rejected several theories before deciding that she was definitely hearing a mountain lion attacking a deer. There was a catlike character to the scream, and she could think of no other big mammal that could make such a large racket, except a human. Then she realized that she was hearing words mixed in with the sounds. There was a long scream, and then the word "help," and another long scream and the words, "Mommy, Mommy."

Her lanky husband stirred in the sleeping bag and Janet helped him awake with a brisk shove. "What made that noise?" Robert Klein said.

"I don't know," Janet said. "Listen!"

After a few seconds, the screaming began again, and this time the words were more distinct.

"Why, it's a child having a nightmare!" Robert said.

"But there's no child in the campground."

"They might have come in after we went to sleep."

Once again, the screaming started, but now it sounded farther away, as though the child were running down the slope of the broad bench of the campground. Then there was one long scream and silence.

The Kleins had no idea what to do; the bright sliver of incandescent moon had gone down behind the mountain, and the geologist and his schoolteacher wife sat together looking into the wall of night, as though waiting for someone to come out of the void and make everything clear. The sounds did

not resume. Robert Klein looked at his watch; it was twelve
fifty.

∞

If there was anything of which young Donald Gullett was
certain when he crawled into his sleeping bag alongside the
trail cabin, it was that he was going to enjoy a long and deep
and dreamless sleep. He had hiked something like twenty
miles that day, and another twenty miles the day before, and
his body throbbed with fatigue. He should not have stayed
up to see the bear come into sight behind the chalet; this had
kept him up till ten or ten thirty; so instead of planning to
continue his international hike at dawn, he simply decided to
sleep out his fatigue and awaken when he awakened, even if
it was some disgustingly late hour of the morning, like seven
or seven thirty.

But now it was almost one o'clock in the morning, and
Gullett was lying in his sleeping bag, looking at his watch
and wondering what had awakened him. It took him a few
seconds to recall that he was camped 500 yards below Granite
Park Chalet and that he was in the middle of a long hike from
Glacier National Park across into Canada and back again. He
heard a noise but thought he was dreaming, and was surprised
when he rolled over on his side to see someone standing at the
foot of his sleeping bag. As he watched sleepily, Gullett saw the
dimly outlined figure slump to its knees, then fall flat. Gullett
looked closely into the eyes of a teenage boy and recognized
Roy Ducat. Young Ducat was alternately giggling and bab-
bling, and Gullett realized that he was in shock. "A bear got a
hold of me," the boy was saying. "I tried playing dead, but it
didn't help. He dragged her off in the brush. You have to go
after her! Oh, please, forget about me! The bear dragged her
away. Can't somebody go and find her?"

Everything had happened in seconds, and Gullett was still
not entirely awake. He slid out of his sleeping bag and said to
himself, "This guy can't be real." To the boy, he said simply,

"You've got to be kidding me." But then he saw that the boy's arm was dangling as though it had been wrenched out of the socket, and blood stains were creeping along the upper pant legs, and all at once Donald Gullett was wide awake and running toward the chalet for help.

"Wait!" the younger boy shouted. "Come back! Don't leave me here. Take me to the others! "

Gullett helped the boy crawl and lurch toward the Kleins' camp about thirty feet away. All the way along the painful journey, Roy kept repeating, "The bear got the girl! It got the girl! Somebody has to help her! The bear dragged her away!" and he repeated words like these when the two of them reached the Kleins.

By now, there were no doubts about what had happened or about the fact that a dangerous bear was loose in the area, and everyone headed for the safety of the trail cabin. It was securely locked. Roy had begun to tremble violently, and Gullett wrapped the wounded boy in his own goose-down mummy bag and laid him gently on the level ground.

"Get up on the roof!" Gullett said to Janet.

"No," she said, "not without Bob."

Robert Klein, who had been gathering up clothes and boots and a flashlight, came puffing up to the side of the trail cabin and helped his wife climb the jutting logs to the tin roof. "Aren't you coming up?" Klein asked Gullett.

"No," the 19-year-old Californian said. "If the bear comes back, I'll be down here with Roy. You can be signaling for help."

On top of the cabin, Robert Klein remembered that danger signals came in threes, and he began blinking the weak flashlight toward the chalet high on the hill. It seemed no time at all before the beam grew weak, along with the couple's hopes. Robert flashed the light around the area a few times, but there was no sign of the bear, and once the beam caught Gullett and the wounded boy, lying just beneath the wall. "How is he?" Robert asked.

"Bad," Gullett said. "He can't walk now."

"If nobody's awake to help us," Janet Klein said softly to her husband, "he'll die from loss of blood." Hardly had she uttered the words when they began to see flickerings of light from the chalet. Someone was up and around, and Robert Klein flashed frantically in triplicate. Soon, a voice came booming down the mountainside, asking, "Is everything OK?" Robert Klein shouted back with all his strength, "No!"

∞

As the little group waited for the help that they now knew was on its way, Roy Ducat slipped in and out of panic but never out of consciousness, and he remembered clearly what had happened. He had been sleeping soundly when all at once he had heard Julie telling him to play dead. While he was still trying to figure out what she was talking about, a single blow from a huge paw knocked both of them five feet away on the ground, and the air was full of an unpleasant smell, as though a dozen dirty sheep dogs had come in from the rain. Roy had landed on his stomach, and out of the corner of his eye, he could see Julie a few feet away. Then he felt something bite deeply into his right shoulder and scrape against the bone, and with a tremendous exercise of his will, he neither cried out nor moved. The biting stopped, and Roy opened his eyes long enough to make out the shadow of a bear standing on all fours above the helpless girl and tearing at her body. He shut his eyes tightly in time to feel the bear return, plant its feet firmly in the small of his back, and begin snapping its teeth into his left arm and the backs of both his legs, just below the buttocks. Still he remained silent, and once again the bear returned to the girl.

Now Roy could hear bones crunching and Julie screaming out, "It hurts!" and "Someone help us!" He realized that the girl's outcries were receding down the hill, and he thought that the bear must be carrying her off. When the screaming stopped, he jumped to his feet and ran uphill as fast as he

could, unaware of his own pain, and slumped alongside the
first sleeping bag he saw. All he could think of was Julie Helgeson and her helplessness and his own helplessness in the
face of the attack, and he begged everyone who came into
sight to forget about him and save the girl.

∞

In his own mind, Tom Walton thought he knew exactly what
had happened, and he was not especially happy about it. He
knew that hysterical women were a fact of life, but he wished
that they would stay away from him. The second he had laid
eyes on Janet Klein, he had seen the panic in her face. Walton
wondered why a husband would insist on camping out with
his wife when anybody could see that the woman was stricken
with fright and would have given anything to be safe inside.
"Now look what happened," Tom Walton said to himself. "A
bear comes sniffing around and the woman starts to scream,
and now half the chalet is awake and ten or fifteen of us have
to form a party and go down the trail to bring help."

Now they were all fumbling along the path, with Tom and
a few of the girls from the kitchen staff in the lead. One of the
girls seemed edgy herself–they had all been awakened out
of sound sleep–and she kept repeating shrilly, "What are we
gonna do? What are we gonna do?"

Walton had had a summerful of dealing with this particular
teenage girl, and he knew that she was a potential hysteric
herself and had to be handled firmly. "Shut up and get in line!"
he snapped. "That's what you're gonna do!"

The young chalet keeper counted thirteen besides himself
as they headed down the rocky, shaly path at the lower edge
of the lava flow toward the trail cabin, where a light seemed
to be blinking off and on. First came Walton and the two
girls, and behind them he recognized the man in the Gonzaga
sweatshirt and the Indian, a couple of medical doctors named
Lipinski and Lindan, the ranger-naturalist Joan Devereaux and
her trusty two-way radio, a strong young man from Montana

named Monty Kuka, and several other guests. Steve Pierre said that there was only one thing on Earth that would frighten a crazed bear, and that was fire. With Father Connolly and several helpers, the Indian grabbed up a galvanized metal tub, filled it with scrap wood, set it to blazing, and dragged it with them. One of the guests toward the rear of the line said, "What are we going for?" and a few minutes later said it again. Walton also wondered why so many guests were going, and why the complainers did not just turn around and go back to bed. But he held his temper and continued down the trail.

∞

From the instant that the rescue party rounded the last bend and came upon the scene at the trail cabin, the place exploded into action and confusion, some of it orderly, much of it understandably disorderly and futile. The sight of the young Ducat, pale and blood-streaked and wrapped like a mummy in Don Gullett's blue sleeping bag, dispelled any feeling of lighthearted adventure; every person in the group now knew that a dangerous grizzly was somewhere in the blackness around them. In the flickering light of the blazing tub, Dr. Olgierd Lindan looked at Ducat and asked for a first-aid kit, but it developed that no one in the rescue party had brought one. "I have one," Robert Klein said; he handed it to Lindan, and in a few seconds the doctor from everywhere was applying makeshift compresses and tourniquets to the boy's gaping wounds. The surgeon, John Lipinski, stood by, ready to take over the case as soon as the first-aid was completed. Like everybody else, Lipinski had heard Roy Ducat beg them to find the girl, but he knew that the search for the other victim would have to wait. He was thinking about the triage system of medical priority under which the doctor's first responsibility was to those who can be saved, while those who were beyond help were left to die or treated last. He had learned about triage on a brief tour in Vietnam, and he did not spell out the system now, knowing how brutal it would sound to civilians, but in his own mind he knew that they would have to tend to Roy Ducat first and worry about the girl when Ducat was out of danger.

"Find something to carry him on," Dr. Lindan said over his shoulder, and Monty Kuka and one of the girls ran to the trail cabin and began pounding on the door. When it gave, the frightened girl rushed in and grabbed a butcher knife, but the calm young Kuka remained outside and began ripping down a set of bedsprings that had been nailed across the outside of one of the windows to keep out bears. It came off neatly, and several of the men took handholds on Ducat's sleeping bag and lifted him gently to the middle of the springs.

The weakened boy kept asking about the girl. "Where is she?" he said. "Did you find her yet?" Dr. Lipinski told him to rest and save his strength, and a small party of stretcher bearers under the surgeon's direction began climbing up toward the chalet. Among the group were the geologist Robert Klein, heaving and straining at the awkward load, and his wife, Janet, shining her flashlight under the men's feet so they could find their way.

At the beginning, the stretcher party took the wrong direction, and the Kleins, who had hiked the trail three times earlier in the evening, could not seem to convince anyone that a mistake was being made. Instead of proceeding along the meadow for fifty yards or so before following the trail directly up to the chalet, the stretcher party blasted straight up the lava flow, on the principle that the chalet was above the trail cabin and so the most direct route must be up. "Look," Robert Klein said, "we're not on the trail," but in the general confusion and terror of the night, no one seemed to hear. Soon they began coming to big boulders, locked into the lava, and soon after that they reached a lip of basalt that was impassable. They had to retrace their steps back down the slippery lava flow to the trail, and by the time they came into sight of the chalet, a ten-minute carry had extended into a half hour. The boy was taken inside and placed on one of the dining-room tables, and Dr. Lipinski rolled up his sleeves to go to work.

∞

About half of the original rescue party had remained below at the trail cabin, some of them in the expectation that they would start searching for the girl, others simply to give aid and comfort to Joan Devereaux, who was frantically trying to raise headquarters on her pack-set radio. At first, the 22-year-old woman had pushed all the wrong buttons in her confusion, and when she finally got the technology figured out, she could not remember the park's radio procedure. Rangers had given her a single quick run-through on the tricky equipment, but establishing radio contact in the middle of the night was not a normal part of the work duties of a ranger-naturalist.

Joan remembered that the headquarters call number was 720, and she said over and over, "seven two oh, seven two oh, this is Granite Park Chalet. We have a bear emergency here." When this brought no response, she began repeating the park's emergency code. "Code three emergency!" she said. "Code three emergency! Bear attack! Bear attack! There's been a bear attack up here at Granite Park Chalet!"

Again there was no answer, and the excited young naturalist regretted her lack of familiarity with the equipment that she had never expected to have to use.

"Keep trying," somebody said. "I know their receivers are on because of the fire watch."

"Code three emergency!" the young woman said, and suddenly a clear "ten four" crackled across the still night air in response. The speaker identified himself as Seasonal Ranger Bert Gildart, said he was on his way over the Divide in his patrol car, and instructed Granite Park Chalet to stand by while he contacted headquarters and tried to put the two in touch with each other. Minutes later, another voice, deep and calm and reassuring, came through the speaker. It was Fire Control Officer Gary Bunney, speaking from the park's fire headquarters, known as the Fire Cache, and asking what the trouble was.

Sitting on the ground in the pulsating light from the pot of fire, surrounded by shadowy forms and the menace of an invisible grizzly, Joan Devereaux seemed to become momentarily distraught. She picked up the microphone, brought it almost to her lips, and cried out, "A mauling! We had a mauling! "

Again the calm voice came from the other end. "Granite Park, you are overmodulating. Move the mike away from your mouth!"

But the naturalist only seemed to become more nervous, and she shouted once again, "A mauling! We had a mauling! "

"Ten four," the calm voice returned. "You had a mauling. What do you need? "

Now the nervous girl seemed to calm slightly, and spacing out her words, but still almost shouting, she said, "We-have-a-doctor. We-do-not-need-a-doctor. We-need-medical-supplies."

"Ten four," the calm voice said. "Tell me exactly what supplies you need."

Dr. Lindan took the microphone and began listing what was needed. "Sutures, transfusion apparatus, plasma or whole blood, morphine, gauze...."

Ranger Bunney interrupted and explained that he was not getting the transmission clearly, and Dr. Lindan realized that the combination of his thick European accent and the weak radio signals were confusing the issue. He handed the microphone back to the naturalist and repeated the list to her for relay. When the medical information had been transmitted, Devereaux informed headquarters that there was a possibility that another person had been dragged away by the bear, and Bunney told her that help was en route.

"All right," Dr. Lindan said to the group when the last "ten fours" had been exchanged and the radio again fell silent, "now we go and find the girl." Tom Walton said, "Wait a minute, let's think about it."

Everyone looked toward Joan Devereaux. She was a slip of a girl and barely out of college and no more experienced than anyone else in the party when it came to the special problems of that night, but she was wearing the dark-green uniform of the National Park Service and therefore she was *de jure* the leader. She did not shrink from the task; as the daughter of an Army officer, she knew about chains of command and ladders of responsibility, and she thought for a moment and announced flatly that no one was going to head into the black night and look for the girl; they were going to return to the chalet and wait for professional help. Dr. Lindan said he did not understand. "We must save the girl," he said. The ranger-naturalist replied that it would be a foolhardy move when they did not even know in what direction she had disappeared.

Hurried conversations broke out. Father Connolly sided with Dr. Lindan. "There's no time to stand here arguing," the priest said. "The girl might be bleeding to death while we talk."

The naturalist said that there was no point in risking anyone else's life when help was already on the way.

Father Connolly whispered to his Indian friend, "Is she right? Is it possible the bear could attack us all? "

"Everything is possible with bears," the Indian replied. Father Connolly shook his head in perplexity. He felt a strong impulse to go after the girl, but he did not want to be responsible for any unnecessary loss of life. He asked a few others how they felt, but no one seemed to know his own mind. Only Dr. Lindan stood his ground; he wanted to head into the night at any cost. Tom Walton pointed out that their flashlights were dimming and they could barely see; most of their illumination was coming from the tub of fire tended by the priest and the Indian. Surely it would be better to wait until help arrived and the search for the girl could be carried out in a calm, orderly manner.

Led by Walton and the naturalist, the party turned back toward the trail that led to the chalet. The priest and the Indian had fitted the fire tub with wire handles, and thus they were able to carry it between them without burning their hands or arms. Everyone stayed as close as possible to the fire as they picked their way along the trail, but they had hardly gone fifty feet when Walton suddenly stopped and motioned for silence. They all heard the same sound. It was coming from the left, up on the lava flow, and it sounded exactly like the low woofing noises that the grizzlies had been making all summer to intimidate one another at the garbage dump. "For God's sake, that's the bear!" somebody said.

"Yes," said Tom Walton. "That's the sound they make when they're mad."

Dragging and straining at the tub of fire, the party double-timed up the narrow trail toward the chalet.

Nancy Walton had been sitting on the balcony with some of the other women, listening to a strange sound in the, night. It sounded like a low moaning. Someone had suggested that it might be an owl, but someone else pointed out that owls were rare around Granite Park. It was only later that Nancy and the others realized they had heard the moans of the grizzly's victim.

∞

Roy Ducat was placed gently on a dining-room table, and as the two doctors, Lindan and Lipinski, looked him over, another man came out of the darkness and introduced himself as a physician from Malmstrom Air Force Base. When Joan Devereaux heard the news, she breathed a silent prayer of thanks. Not only were there three doctors in attendance, but Dr. Lipinski's wife was a registered nurse, and except for the fact that there was almost no medical equipment on the premises, there was every chance to hope for the boy's recovery.

As for the girl, Joan told her companions once again what she had been telling herself ever since she had first realized that a young girl was missing. The child was suffering, perhaps dying, but Joan pointed out to the others that a lunatic bear was on the loose, and it would be suicidal for a search party of chalet guests to go out into the black night armed only with a bucket of fire and some kitchen knives. Headquarters had radioed that a helicopter would arrive in twenty or thirty minutes with medical supplies and an armed ranger. The rescue operation would simply have to wait. The young naturalist knew that she had a responsibility not only to the young girl moaning in the woods, but also to the sixty-five people in the chalet who looked to her for direction. She stood firm. And Tom Walton stood firm with her.

While the doctors were working on Ducat in the light of hand-held Coleman lanterns and flashlights, Father Tom Connolly and his Indian friend, Steve Pierre, were trying to recruit a rescue party. Dr. Lindan had stepped back as the surgeon, Lipinski, had taken over the medical procedures, and at the quiet approach of the priest, Dr. Lindan reported softly that the boy was going to survive, and he would like to begin on the rescue of the girl as quickly as possible. Father Connolly agreed and went to round up others. In a few minutes, a party of eight or ten would-be rescuers was ready to depart, but Joan Devereaux intercepted them and told them that a rescue helicopter and an armed ranger would be on the scene within minutes and ordered them to wait. The priest did not want to lose any time; some of the rescue party turned to Tom Walton for support, but Walton said, "No, we're not going. There's an armed ranger coming right in. There's nothing we can do now. The bear could eat us all up. We're not going! "

To himself, Walton remembers saying, "OK, we've got to be realistic about this. There could be fifty of us going down there, and the bear could gobble us all up. And we have no idea where she is. We don't even know where they were sleeping. And all we've got to defend ourselves with is the fire—and if the bear's really riled up, the fire won't stop him. Sure, this man is a priest, and maybe he's got some protection from above, but I'm not so sure that I do. I have no reason to believe that the bear won't eat me and everybody else." And once again, he said aloud, "You're not going! Nobody's going down there! It's stupid!"

With the helicopter due any minute, Walton and the naturalist hastily impressed about twenty chalet guests into duty preparing a landing site. Several days earlier, a helicopter had landed in a flat space behind the chalet, but that had been in broad daylight, and now it was the densest of nights. Joan set some of the guests to work building fires to mark the corners of the site, and Walton ordered others to bring buckets of water in case the fires got away. Several young guests grabbed axes and chopped down a wooden hitching rack that represented a hazard to the helicopter, and others draped warning lanterns on a few big stakes and pipes that could not be moved.

The landing pad was almost ready when the throbbing lights of the helicopter came into sight over the mountains to the south, and Joan took up her station at the two-way radio. She heard a flabbergasted fire guard saying on the air, "Hey, they're building fires down there!" and the comforting voice of Ranger Gary Bunney replying, "That's OK, that's OK, that's OK." As the helicopter moved into position about 500 feet above the landing site, a man came out of the shadows and told the girl ranger that he had flown helicopters and would be glad to help talk the aircraft in. Joan nodded her thanks and radioed to the pilot, "You can see the four fires. Try to land right in the middle of them. It's exactly the same place where you landed the other day."

The helicopter began settling down for the landing; the four corner fires blazed high into the sky, and a wide circle of guests pointed flashlights upward. Suddenly the aircraft zoomed away, and Bunney's voice crackled over the radio,

"We can't see! All that light makes a reflection on the dome and blinds us."

"What should we do?" the naturalist asked.

"Have them point the flashlights down on the ground," Bunney replied, "and put some people in front of the fires to block out the direct light."

Joan issued the new orders in top-sergeant style that surprised herself, and within a few minutes, the helicopter was in another descent, assisted by advices from the former helicopter pilot on the ground and relayed by the girl naturalist. As the aircraft came within range of the fires, embers swirled into the night air, and Walton and his crew of fire watchers rushed with their buckets to track down each tiny glow. Then, with a gentle bump and a whoosh of settling air, the helicopter was down. Even before the rotor had stopped turning, the onlookers could see a man in ranger uniform open the door and run out, cradling a rifle in his arms. Willing hands reached into the aircraft and lifted the medical supplies, and everything was rushed into the improvised operating room.

In the darkness and confusion, someone had mislaid the needle for administering intravenous blood, and when Dr. Lipinski heard that the needle was missing, he recommended that the boy be airlifted immediately to the hospital thirty air miles away in Kalispell. Ducat's wounds were serious but not critical; muscles and tendons had been torn away in his arm, and there were deep lacerations on his legs and back, but the only danger to his life was the loss of blood. Still in Don Gullett's blue mummy bag, the 18-year-old former lifeguard from Ohio was lifted gently to the seat alongside helicopter pilot John Westover and whisked away in the night. All this was completed in ten or fifteen minutes, and at last Joan Devereaux turned to her superior ranger and said, "Now we've got to go find the girl."

Gary Bunney said, "You stay here and handle the radio. I'll take the men and go down."

As the posse of searchers disappeared on the trail to the cabin below, the weary naturalist went inside the chalet dining room to put the radio back on the air. Dr. Lipinski told her, "Let me know when they bring in the girl," and disappeared in the direction of his room. A few women sat around sobbing; their husbands had gone off with the search party. An older woman clomped halfway down the stairs and asked what was causing the gassy smell. "We're making coffee in the kitchen," said Eileen Anderson. "That's probably what you smell." The older woman nodded her head, as though this simple explanation accounted for the helicopter sounds and the medical apparatus in the dining room and the sobbing women and the general air of emergency. She turned and headed back to her bed.

Joan was sitting at one of the dining-room tables, fiddling with the controls of the Motorola radio when a man sat down alongside. She turned and recognized the young Air Force doctor from Malmstrom. "I'm sure you're aware of this already," he said, "but I want to tell you one thing."

"What's that?" the ranger asked.

"The boy was in bad shape," the young doctor said gently, "but the girl is going to be much worse."

Joan Devereaux nodded her head and told him that she understood. Off in a corner, a man was saying to his wife, "I wouldn't go down there. If those damned fools want to go down there and get caught by a bear, let them go. I'm not gonna risk my life."

His wife said, "Well, at least be quiet about it."

Another man was explaining in vivid detail how the rescue should be carried out, closing his explanatory lecture with the words, "That's exactly the way it should be done."

"Then why aren't you out doing it?" a voice asked.

"Are you kidding?" the man asked.

"My husband shouldn't be down there," a sobbing woman said. "His heart isn't good. I'm afraid they'll be bringing him back on a stretcher." Another woman moved over to comfort her, and the two sat with their arms around each other, crying and dabbing at their eyes. Joan turned the volume control to maximum and walked to the window. Far down the slope, she could see the glow of the washtub, surrounded by bobbing points of light like fireflies. A muffled shouting came up the mountain, as though a football game were in progress a mile away, and Joan realized that the men were making noises to scare off the bear. She turned to the radio and told headquarters that the rescue operation was under way.

∞

Sometime between two and three in the morning, Denise Huckle found herself awake and listening intently to a splashing sound that was coming from the shallow water alongside the camp at Trout Lake. Squirt pushed himself up on his front paws and peered into the night toward the sound, and when a low growl began to issue from the puppy's throat, Denise grabbed him and stuffed him under her sleeping bag. She thought she could make out the silhouette of a bear, and she did not want Squirt to antagonize the animal. When the sounds seemed to move out of the water and down toward the original camp, Denise awoke the others and told them what she had heard. After a few minutes of silence, the Noseck brothers scrambled out and rebuilt the fire, by now only a bed of dull embers. They set the sack of cookies on the edge of a driftwood log, fanned up the fire once again, and returned to their bags. Within a few minutes, the bear had walked to the edge of the camp, grabbed up the cookie bag in a huge paw, and disappeared. Paul Dunn, the deepest of the sleepers, was up now, and the five frightened campers decided to lie awake, feed the fire, and wait for dawn. It was 3 o'clock; first light would be about 5:30 or 6. Paul Dunn inched his sleeping bag closer to the roaring fire but inched it back when his toes became too hot.

Once again, the bear began splashing in the shallow water

below the camp, and almost simultaneously a woofing sound seemed to come from the woods above. For a few minutes, the companions of the night discussed whether bears attacked in packs or couples and finally decided that they did not. By 4 a.m., the noises had stopped, and most of the campers had pulled the bags over their heads and gone back to sleep.

Denise comforted Squirt, imprisoned for his own safety under the sleeping bag, and tried to stay awake. Dawn was not far off. More than once, Denise thought she heard noises around the edge of the campsite, and each time she patted and stroked the dog to keep him from making a sound. Except for the single low growl earlier when the bear had been wading around the edge of Trout Lake, Squirt's behavior had been perfect, but there was no doubt that the dog's scent was on everything in the camp, and especially on the two girls, Denise and Michele, who had spent more time than the others babying him in their arms. Denise tucked her pet farther under the bag till he was completely hidden.

It was 4:30, and the fire had fallen to low flames and embers again when she heard a splash and narrowed her eyes to peer into the night and saw a bear coming at a lope straight from the shoreline toward the center of the camp. When the bear was four or five feet away and she could make out its head and upper body clearly, Denise pulled the sleeping bag over herself and Squirt, just as the dog began a high-pitched squeal. Lying perfectly still inside the warm bag, the terrified girl heard a ripping noise that sounded like shredding canvas, but then there was a silence broken only by the deep breathing and grunting of the grizzly. She held Squirt tightly in her arms and felt his trembling mingle with her own. She tried to keep the dog from bawling out its fright, as the bear sniffed rapidly at the bag.

Paul Dunn woke up and peeped from his own sleeping bag to see the huge wet form of the bear standing next to him. Noiselessly, the boy slithered into his bag and tried to remain absolutely still. He heard the bear making more sniffing sounds, and suddenly he realized that the sniffs were getting closer and closer. Then something crunched into his sleeping bag and took a firm grip on his sweatshirt. Instinctively, the boy threw back the flap of the bag and scrambled to his feet, slamming into the bear in the process and shouting to no one in particular, "The goddamn bear tore my shirt!" When the grizzly reared up on its hind feet as though to attack, Paul dashed to a tree and climbed thirty or forty feet in a matter of seconds, ripping and cutting his chest and his legs on the desperate ascent. When he reached the safety of the top, he looked down and saw the bear circling lazily below.

Lying in bags side by side, Denise and Ron Noseck saw the bear amble over to Paul Dunn's tree, a few feet outside the semicircle of campers, and Ron decided that the time had come to run for trees of their own. "We have to get out of here!" he yelled, and Denise replied, "I can't. I've got to undo the collar around Squirt's neck." Once again, Noseck told his girlfriend to run, and when she did not move, the 21-year-old dental student yanked the girl full-length from her sleeping bag and gave her a shove toward the southern end of the lake. The couple ran about fifty yards in the direction of the original camp, and as they ran, they heard Paul Dunn shouting down from his treetop. He seemed to be telling Ray and Michele to get out of their sleeping bags and make a break for it, but in their own headlong flight down the lakeline, Denise and Ron could not be sure. They reached a slight incline, and as they stopped, gasping for breath, the puppy came bounding up. Ron boosted the girl up a tree, threw the dog after her, and shinnied up a tree of his own. Neither one could see distinctly to the new camp fifty yards away, but they could still hear Paul Dunn shouting, and they added their own cries to the pandemonium. "Get out!" they yelled toward the camp. "Find a tree!"

From his observation point almost directly above the camp, Paul Dunn saw everything that happened within the small circle of reddish light thrown off by the dying fire. He saw Ron and Denise run down the shoreline, followed by the puppy, and then he saw the grizzly walk toward Ray Noseck's sleeping bag and begin sniffing rapidly. When the bear turned momentarily toward Michele's bag, Ray came out of his own as though shot from a gun and headed down the lake toward Denise and Ron, shouting as he ran, "Get out of your bag and run for it! "

Paul hollered at Michele, "Get out! Get out! Unzip and get out! "

The bear clamped its jaws on the side of the sleeping bag, and Paul heard the girl begin to scream. When the animal raked the bag with its claws, Paul heard Michele cry out, "He's ripping my arm! "

"Michele!" Paul shouted. "Get out of your bag! Run and climb a tree! "

"I can't," the girl screamed. "He's got the zipper!"

Then the defenseless girl shouted, "He's got my arm.... My arm is gone! Oh, my God, I'm dead! "

Paul Dunn saw the bear lift the sleeping bag in its mouth and drag it out of the circle of fire and up the hillside into the darkness. He heard a sound like bones crunching and shouted down the lake to the other three, "He's pulling her up the hill!" and then, "She's dead! She's dead!"

In the hysteria of the moment, it seemed to the 16-year-old boy that he must get dressed and join his friends, and when he figured that the bear and its helpless bundle were at least fifty yards up the hill, he scrambled down the trunk and slipped his trousers over his underclothes. Then he sprinted along the lake to the others and climbed another tree, and the four survivors of the attack comforted one another and waited for the dawn. It came at 6 a.m., an hour and a half after the attack, and while Ray attended to Denise and the dog, the two younger men ran back to the campsite and gathered up shoes and jackets.

They listened for any sounds coming from the dark woods that might indicate Michele was still alive. From somewhere up the hill in the direction the bear had taken, Ron was sure he could hear the sound of bones being snapped. The four terrified campers yanked on their shoes and ran down the trail toward the turnoff that led up and over Howe Ridge. Denise thought she saw the bear in the brush as they ran, but she said nothing, and two hours later, after running and stumbling and lurching four miles up and down the 2,000 feet of hill, the campers burst out on the road that ran from Going-to-the-Sun Highway along the northern edge of Lake McDonald to Kelly's Camp. A fisherman and his wife had parked at the trailhead and were just starting to hike in, but they took one look at the panicky group coming out and urged them into their car. When they pulled up at the path that led to the lake and the small ranger station, the four refugees from Trout Lake asked their benefactors to keep the dog in the car. Then they rushed off to tell their story to the ranger.

∞

Fire Control Officer Gary Bunney and his rescue party had begun their mercy mission at 2:45 a.m., almost exactly two hours after the attack in the Granite Park campground. Since they were not sure where the young couple had been camping, the rescuers decided to go straight down the path to the trail cabin and try to fan out from there in the general direction of the campground. Bunney was in the lead, a powerful miner's lamp strapped to his forehead and his finger lightly touching the safety of his .300 Winchester Magnum. Right behind him were the Indian, Steve Pierre; the innkeeper, Tom Walton; the geologist, Robert Klein; the priest, Tom Connolly; the doctor, Olgierd Lindan, the strong young man from Montana, Monty Kuka; the hiker from California, Don Gullett; the anonymous former pilot who had assisted in the landing; and six or eight others. They had not gone more than 100 yards downtrail when they had to step over bear droppings, fresh and steaming in the cool night air, and Gary Bunney slowed the pace for a short consultation. He adjusted his head lamp so that it would shine dead ahead, and he said, "If the bear comes into sight, we'll be in a tough spot. There's only one chance, and that's for you to shine your lights right on him and *keep* them shining on him, because I can't hit him in this kind of darkness, and whether you know it or not, a grizzly can move. And remember this: Stay back! Don't go moving out ahead of me, because if you do, we'll just be one big jumble of bodies out there, and I won't know where I can shoot and where I can't, and a lot of people could get hurt."

As the group continued toward the trail cabin, stepping gingerly across more fresh sign, Walton focused his five-cell flashlight out ahead of the ranger, but he could see that even this powerful torch was dimming after several hours of use. Behind him was a small amount of diffused reddish light coming from the fire tub dragged by the priest and fed by some of the others, but not enough to shine more than a few feet into the bushes and scraggly trees of the timberline area. Some of the men were keeping up a steady shouting to frighten the bear, and a few of the voices had turned hoarse and quavery. "Whoa, bear!" one man shouted tremulously. "Whoa, bear!" Walton had to admire the man, whoever he was. He was plainly stricken with terror but nevertheless proceeding down the trail to provide his share of help to a suffering human being.

Walton and a few of the others toward the front of the line began making sounds; their primary mission was to find the missing girl, not to kill the bear, and the best way to find the girl was to avoid a diversionary episode with the bear and the possibility of even more bloodshed. The innkeeper thought about the grim differences between this trip toward the trail cabin and the one a few hours earlier. Now he had seen the massive rips and punctures in young Ducat's body; the menace of the bear was, therefore, no longer an imaginary one.

Real blood had been shed, real tissue torn, and somewhere in the night that enveloped them, the instrument of damage was running at large, perhaps following them soundlessly. Tom played his light from side to side, but there was nothing except a few stunted trees to the left and the gray-black of the lava flow stretching all the way up to pinpoints of stars on the right.

When the party had almost reached the trail cabin, Walton asked for silence; they were at the same place where bear woofings had been heard on the trip up. When the last "Whoa, bear!" died down in the stillness of the night, Walton and the others began to hear the same woofings up the hill, and all at once the young innkeeper knew what was causing the sound. He explained to the others that the noise was coming from the water ram, a device that was installed in the stream up above and was a part of the chalet's pumping system. He apologized for frightening some of them earlier, but in all the excitement and terror of the attacks, he had forgotten about the water ram.

At the trail cabin, the searchers stopped for another conference. They had an idea where the attack had taken place, but no one knew in which direction the girl had been dragged. Steve Pierre said he doubted that a bear would carry a human for more than 100 yards or so and suggested that they go to the campground and locate the couple's campsite and spread out from there. Once again, the armed ranger took the lead, and this time he kept the Indian and Robert Klein just behind him. Klein had heard the girl's screams; he could steer them toward the place where Ducat and Julie Helgeson had been sleeping.

The couple's little camp turned out to be in the middle of the cleared area where the Park Service had hauled in material for tables and toilets and benches but had not yet put them together. On the ground lay a sign: "GRANITE PARK CAMPGROUND." Sleeping bags and shoes and camp gear were strewn about, and there was an indistinct trail of blood heading up the hill toward the trail cabin, and a pool of blood soaked into a trampled patch of false hellebore a few feet down the hill. "Didn't the boy say he came uphill all the way?" Steve Pierre asked Don Gullett.

"Yes," Gullett said.

The Indian and Bunney reached the same conclusion at once. "This must be the girl's blood down here," the ranger said. "The bear must have carried her downhill."

This deduction narrowed the arc of the search area to 180 degrees, and the group spread out and began to move haltingly down the mountain. Instead of shouting "Whoa, bear!" they were calling, "Julie, Julie, where are you, Julie?" But the fact of the bear's existence was uppermost in all their minds. Tom Walton choked back a rising sense of panic and moved just behind Bunney, expecting the bear to come charging out of the brush at any second and knock them all to the ground before the ranger could get off a shot. Some of the men were banging on pots to add to the noise, and Father Connolly and an assistant continued to drag the fire tub along the ground while others ran around trying to find scrap wood to keep the blaze high. Now and then, an ember would bounce out of the tub, and someone would stomp it out and rush to rejoin the search line. No one wanted to be alone, but neither could they stay in a big mass and hope to find the missing girl. So the line expanded and contracted with the courage of the men and the menace of the night.

Now the Indian called out that he had found a trail of blood specks along the asters and the glacier lilies, and the group knotted up behind him. Within a few yards, he leaned over and picked up a bloody purse, empty except for a single dollar bill. The Indian increased his pace down the slope below the bench, and several times Bunney had to tell him to slow down and get behind the gun. The men followed the Indian far down the mountain, out of sight of the chalet light, and then the bloody trail disappeared. "I'm sorry," Steve Pierre said, "but it's gone. We'll have to spread out again."

The searchers had traveled the length of a football field from the campsite; there were neither trails nor cleared areas nor signs to guide them, and they widened reluctantly and began creeping down the slope trying to cut the trail of blood again. Their flashlights had been off and on for two hours, and now they barely illuminated the ground. The men made more noise than ever; it had occurred to more than a few of them that the girl might be lying dead just a few feet away with the bear standing guard, and they had heard what grizzlies will do to protect a kill.

The line of search had dropped down another twenty yards when an alien sound began to intrude itself into the noisemaking. "Quiet!" Bunney begged, and slowly the group brought itself to order. From off to the left and slightly farther down the slope, they heard a muted cry for help. At the sound of the tiny voice, the strung-out searchers reacted as a single person. Now it was as though there were no bear, as though the suffering girl were the only reality on the dark flank of the mountain. Now they were adult men listening to a suffering human, and they dashed headlong, tripping over logs and bushes, toward the small, weak voice.

Bunney, Tom Walton, and Steve Pierre were the first to reach the scene. The girl lay on her face in a hollow. Her body was ripped and torn, and she was covered with blood, and to the first observers, it appeared impossible that she could be alive. But when Dr. Lindan came running up and dropped to his knees over the prostrate form, the girl began to move her lips, and then everyone could hear her say, "It hurts."

"Get something to carry her on," Dr. Lindan said over his shoulder, and Monty Kuka and Don Gullett and a few others dashed toward the trail cabin, 250 yards away, to rip off another bedspring. Dr. Lindan examined the girl. Somehow she had managed to roll her blood-drenched blouse into a ball and slip it under her head for a pillow. She wore cutoff blue jeans, and there were puncture holes and long rips in the back of her pant legs. The girl's hair was matted with blood and dirt. Between the hand and the elbow of her right arm, there appeared to be nothing but bone, and a foam of blood was oozing from holes in both left and right thorax regions.

Dr. Lindan recognized these "sucking wounds" as an immediate threat to the girl's life: One lung was already collapsed, and the punctures made it impossible for her to breathe normally. Her facial and neck muscles were contorting and throbbing as they worked to replace the oxygen that was hissing out of the holes in her chest faster than it could be replaced. Quickly, Dr. Lindan placed compresses on the holes and bandaged them as tightly as he could. When he started to turn the girl over gently, she said, "Cold, cold," and Dr. Lindan ripped off his own shirt and covered her. Most of the others removed their jackets and shirts, and soon the wounded girl was lying under a layer of borrowed clothing. The doctor called for more shirts and began tearing them into long strips, and while the crew was still en route for the bedspring stretcher, he bandaged the girl's wounds and tried to stanch the flow of blood. By now, despite the profusion of coagulated blood all over the scene, there was little fluid coming from the gaping holes; it appeared that in the two hours since the attack, most of the girl's blood supply had drained away into the earth. To Dr. Lindan, it was a miracle that she had managed to stay alive so long.

Tom Walton was one of those who had ripped off shirts and jackets and sweaters and awaited the doctor's next command, but suddenly he found he was unable to look on any longer. He felt that he would faint if he did not sit down, and he staggered backward and landed heavily on a rock. After a few minutes of holding his head in his hands, he looked up at the back of the crowd congregated around the scene and wondered why a few of the men still wore not only their shirts but their parkas. He figured that they must not have heard the request from the doctor. Then his attention was carried to a slightly built man of about 30 or 35 with a crew cut and a mustache, studying something in his hand. While the stricken Walton sat and watched dazedly, the mousy-looking little man pushed his way through the ring of onlookers, dropped to a squatting position, and snapped a picture. It occurred to Walton that he should stand up and smash both camera and man, but he decided to vomit instead.

∞

Under the energetic direction of Joan Devereaux, the dining area of the chalet had been turned into an emergency room. At first, some important items had been missing, but the young ranger-naturalist refused to believe that the medical specialists back at headquarters could have left out anything as vital as intravenous needles and morphine, and she practically ripped the packages apart inch by inch looking for them. Now she held the missing items triumphantly in the light of the lanterns that hung from rafters to illuminate the place, and several women joined her in setting up the makeshift operating arena. They pulled two long dining tables together and covered them with sheets, connected the plasma bottle with its tube and needle, and made everything as neat and clean as anyone could make a rough mountainside chalet at 3:30 in the morning. When someone reported that a slow procession of shouting men appeared to be approaching up the mountain, Joan awoke Dr. Lipinski. The surgery was as ready as humanly possible. "Please leave now," she told the knot of women sitting at the other tables. "We'll let you know how everything is going." Some of the women left; some remained.

As soon as Julie Helgeson was transferred from the bedsprings to the operating table, the doctor gave her an intramuscular shot for pain and began removing the first-aid bandages that covered the severe sucking wound of the left thorax. The puncture was about an inch and a half wide. Dr. Lipinski placed his hand across it and realized that there was no way to improvise a perfect seal. Indeed the surgeon doubted that the problem could have been solved in the operating room of a major hospital; too much time had passed. As he hurriedly applied a dressing to the wound and tried to cover over each pinpoint of air leakage, he saw that the girl's body was calling on the last reserves of respiration: Muscles in the neck and the intercostals between the ribs were standing out clearly as they tried to assist primary muscles of respiration like the diaphragm and the abdominal muscles, and still there was that terrible suck-suck of the air being lost through the hole. Dr. Lipinski looked at the girl's face. It was almost the only undamaged part of her. He could see the signs of the terrible fight her body was making. As she fought to get air, her mouth opened and her teeth showed, and the muscles in her cheeks throbbed with effort.

Occasionally, Dr. Lipinski glanced around to see what the others were doing. With the almost soldierly discipline that well-trained physicians bring to their work, each man had found a role: Lipinski, the surgeon, working on the chest wounds; Lindan, the internist, splinting the girl's ruined arm with two heavy pieces of cardboard; and the Air Force doctor, the youngest of the three, improving the dressings that had been applied in the field. Dr. Lipinski raised a gentle, admonitory hand in the young physician's direction, signaling him not to try to do too much with the dressings. The surgeon operated on a number of established precepts, one of which was the triage system, and another of which was the principle of "skillful neglect," which taught that if one could do next to nothing to improve a medical situation, sometimes it was better to do nothing at all. In this case, he felt that the dressings had better be left alone, but he communicated his instructions to the young doctor as gently as possible, realizing that the Air Force medic was trying as mightily as any of them to save the victim's life.

For the first several minutes of the emergency procedure, the tall surgeon had allowed himself to believe that the patient had a chance for survival, but as he took inventory of the injuries, he realized that he had been optimistic. In addition to the mangled arm and the punctured thorax, there were gashes and cuts all over the girl's body, perhaps made by the timber and rocks she had been dragged across, and the injuries to the upper legs turned out to be more than cuts and scrapes: There were whole sections of flesh chewed away.

Lipinski ordered his teenage daughter, Terese, to hold the flashlight close while he began a cutdown to try to find a vein in the girl's ankle, but no matter how deeply he probed, he found nothing but chalky white flesh. The loss of blood had been extreme, and now it appeared that the veins were collapsed. The surgeon abandoned the ankle and cut into the wrist, and after much effort, he succeeded in finding an uncollapsed vein and inserting the needle. The plasma bottle was hung from a rafter high above, and the precious fluid began seeping into the girl's circulatory system.

Tom Walton had been standing on the outer fringe of the medical team that consisted mostly of Joan Devereaux, Terese Lipinski, a helpful member of the rescue team named Riley Johnson, all of whom had been holding lights, Lipinski's wife, Ann, the registered nurse, and the three doctors themselves, but there seemed nothing that Walton could contribute to the operation, so he headed out to help keep the fires blazing for the incoming helicopter. As he left, he saw the priest, still wearing his Gonzaga jacket with the black and white piping, take up a station at the end of the table and begin whispering to the girl.

The presence of Father Connolly puzzled some of the medical staff who did not recognize him as a priest or did not know who he was, but his easy confidence quickly made it plain that he was a person skilled in the art of bringing spiritual succor to the suffering. The balding young man began speaking of

God's love and concern, and the girl, momentarily at rest, seemed to respond. "The doctors are doing everything that can be done to take care of you," the priest said, "and you know that God will watch over you and take care of you."

Weakly the girl said, "Yes, I know He will."

Father Connolly looked down the table at Dr. Lipinski and, without saying a word, asked the surgeon if the girl was going to live, and with the merest side-to-side motion of his head, Dr. Lipinski told the priest that the end was very near. "Can you get some water?" the priest asked Ann Lipinski, and the nurse rushed away toward the kitchen. When she returned, she cautioned Father Connolly not to let the patient try to sip the water, but simply to wet a rag and let her suck at it. The priest said he wanted the water for another purpose.

"You know that God loves you, don't you?" he said gently, but the girl was no longer able to speak. The priest took her hand and said, "God loves you, did you know that?" She squeezed his hand with the lightest of pressure. He asked if she had been baptized, but she did not answer, and he told her that he was going to baptize her conditionally. In a soft voice, just above a whisper, he told the girl that he would trace the sign of the cross on her forehead, and if she had not been baptized before, this would serve as a baptism. While the doctors watched in the soft glow of the yellowing flashlights, the priest annointed the girl with water, traced the sign of the cross, and whispered, "I baptize you in the name of the Father, and the Son, and the Holy Spirit." He gave her absolution for her sins, and when he said the Act of Contrition, they all saw to their amazement that the girl seemed to be trying to follow with her lips. Then suddenly her breathing became loud and shallow; she hiccuped once or twice and lay silent. It was 4:12 a.m.

∞

When the helicopter took off from the improvised pad behind Granite Park Chalet and blinked away in the night with the body of Julie Helgeson strapped to its right landing tray, most of the participants in the long ordeal stirred and watered the outdoor fires and returned to the dining room, where coffee and hot chocolate were still being served by Mrs. Eileen Anderson and the kitchen staff. For a while, nothing was said, but then the busy ranger-naturalist, Joan Devereaux, entered the room and said that she had an announcement to make. In the morning at about 9 a.m., she told the hushed group, breakfast would be served, and as soon after breakfast as possible, they would hike out of Granite Park Chalet en masse. She told them that she had selected the Alder Trail for the exit route; it was about a mile longer than the Loop Trail, but slightly less steep and also less likely to harbor grizzlies. If anyone wanted to go out by another exit, that was their privi- lege. A few people grumbled that they had their own plans, some to go over Swiftcurrent Pass toward Many Glacier, and one or two to go back out the long, flat Highline Trail under the Garden Wall. Joan told them the decision was theirs, but there was safety in numbers, and anyone who wanted to join the regular exodus was welcome. She suggested that they get a few hours' sleep, and while the guests moved off one by one toward their rooms, she busied herself washing the operating tables and cleaning up the medical supplies hanging useless in the light of the Coleman lanterns and candles. She wanted to make the dining room as neat and tidy as possible by morn- ing, so that it would seem less oppressive. By 5 a.m., the task was completed, and the 22-year-old ranger-naturalist lay on her bed in her full uniform and realized that she had never had an instant during the long night to be afraid. Now the fear flowed over her, and she was unable to sleep.

∞

When all the cots and mattresses and sleeping bags had once again been dragged onto the dining-room floor and ev- eryone else was either asleep or trying to sleep, Tom Walton and his wife, Nancy, and their close friend Helen Lundgren tiptoed to the front porch of the chalet for a final cigarette, and off to one side, sitting quietly in the shadows, they saw Father Connolly and Steve Pierre. The two men from Spokane were in canvas chairs, and they seemed to be staring into the night in the direction of the campground below. Walton and the two girls did not disturb them; the priest and the Indian appeared to be deep in thoughts of their own, and neither of them spoke.

Tom had the portable radio, and now that there was nothing more to be done for the bear's victims, he signaled headquarters and asked if someone would contact his boss, Concessioner Ross Luding, and give him a full report. "If you can contact Ross," Walton said into the microphone, "tell him we had a bear attack up here."

"Don't say anything more about the incident!" the voice from headquarters snapped back. "We'll call Ross Luding for you. But don't say any more on the radio about the incident!" A few minutes later, the voice of Ross Luding crackled out of the two-way radio speaker. "I'll be there in a few hours," Luding announced, and Tom Walton acknowledged the message and signed the mountainside station off the air. When the last cigarettes had been smoked, the three walked softly inside the chalet and headed for their beds. "Wait a minute," Walton whispered to his wife. He pulled out his flashlight and flicked the beam on the blackboard menu that hung next to the kitchen door. Swiftly and noiselessly, he picked up the chalk and made a change in the wording. Instead of "Grizzly burgers, all sold out," he wrote, "Goat burgers, all sold out." The young innkeeper cursed himself for not making the change earlier.

∞

As he lay in bed unable to sleep that Saturday night, August 12, Seasonal Ranger Leonard Landa could not rid himself of a nagging feeling of frustration. This was the fourth season in the park for the 26-year-old English teacher and, in almost all ways, it had been the most difficult. Supposedly, he was to watch over the upper end of Lake McDonald and the nearby highway and dirt roads and to see that everything went smoothly at Trout and Arrow lakes, a two-hour hike over Howe Ridge. But now the summer season was three-quarters over, and Ranger Landa's acquaintance with Trout and Arrow lakes had been less than nodding. Early in the summer, he had hiked over the ridge and carried out an inspection visit, finding the campsites and the shelter cabin and the trail registers in order. Everything had appeared in such good order, in fact, that Ranger Landa had not returned to either lake. There were several reasons. One was that Leonard Landa, a tall, apple-cheeked North Dakotan with blue eyes, light-brown hair, and a strong profile like a movie ranger, had neither the time nor the inclination to hike over Howe Ridge and did not mind saying so. In the past, rangers stationed at Lake McDonald had only to draw horses from the park's pool of stock and ride comfortably into Trout and Arrow lakes on their inspections. But this year, there was a new system, and horses were harder to get, and anyway Landa doubted if he would have found time for the field trips even if a whole stable had been at his disposal. All week long, the tourists would rap on the door of the little ranger station, asking for fire permits, advice, assistance, and guidance, and the ranger had to stay put. To add to his work load, the Park Service had made its usual batch of transfers, and much of the summer was spent breaking in new men, including a new district ranger. There was hardly any time for working in the field, especially when one was already doing the work of two or three men.

Then there was the matter of the bear. Twice Ranger Landa had gone to Kelly's Camp to assist in setting up a trap for the marauding animal, but nothing had come of that, and now he had been hearing about a similar bear, if not the same specimen, chasing and harassing campers at Trout and Arrow lakes. He supposed he should hike in and see if he could find the animal, but then again, there were certain complications. Undoubtedly, the bear should be destroyed, but did the Park Service really want him to put a bullet in the grizzly's skull? The order had been out for a month to shoot the animal, but Ranger Landa knew that some orders were different from others. The chief ranger, in his second summer in the park, was known to be extremely sympathetic to the plight of the grizzlies, and Landa could not rid himself of the feeling that the order to kill the bear was merely a formality that park officialdom hoped would not be carried out. Twice Landa had conferred with one of his superiors about the troublesome bear, and twice he had been told to wait and see. Then the execution order had been issued, but headquarters had done nothing to implement it. As usual, the matter was left up to the ranger in the field, in this case Leonard Landa. Several times he had picked up his .300 H&H Magnum and driven up to Kelly's Camp to look for the bear, but the residents told him that the animal always bolted up the hill as soon as the sound of the engine reached its ears. There remained an almost certain way to eliminate the bear, and that was to pack into Trout Lake, set up camp, and stay until the bear came sniffing around, but that could take three or four days, and Ranger Landa was hard-pressed to find three or four hours, let alone days.

Tossing against his pillow in the cabin that he shared with his wife and two sons, the handsome young man said to himself that the problem of this particular bear would have to be met squarely sooner or later, and not by that vague organization known as the National Park Service, but by himself, Seasonal Ranger Leonard Landa. It was embarrassing that the animal had made the newspapers at least twice: once a few weeks ago when Steve Ashlock and John Cook had been chased, and again just two days earlier, when Girl Scout Troop 367 had been forced to flee over the ridge. Nothing official had come to Landa from his superiors as a result of the Ashlock-

Cook article, but he had heard through the grapevine that the discussions at headquarters had been long and loud after the bear's picture had been printed on page 1 of the *Daily Inter Lake*. This time, he had expected a blast from the chief ranger and a demand for a complete explanation of the fact that the bear was still running loose after misbehaving for an entire summer. But there was no official reaction whatever. As he said to himself wonderingly, "No one called and said, 'Leonard, about that bear up there, we're getting a lot of kickback, we'd better go shoot it.' It's just like the Army. You don't make a decision yourself, you let it get to the top and then they talk about it for three or four months. But you can't just go out and plug a bear that's fooling around a campground. Seems like the Park Service feels that as long as we don't have anything serious or it doesn't look like it's gonna develop into a big problem, then don't shoot the bear."

So on this Saturday night, August 12, 1967, the Trout Lake bear remained unshot, and Landa knew that it would have to remain unshot at least for the foreseeable future. A dry lightning storm had sent more than 100 hot strikes lashing into the parched forest, and every available ranger was out on the fire lines. Seasonal Ranger Leonard Landa, one of the lowest men on the park's totem pole, was in charge of the whole district; all his immediate superiors were out in the field, and even the two fire fighters normally assigned to his ranger station were gone. To Landa, it seemed a fitting end for the summer. The overworked were to be overworked some more. He went to sleep on the thought.

Sometime after midnight, Landa realized that the shortwave radio next to his bed was handling more than the normal whispered communications of early morning, and he reached across and increased the volume. He heard a female voice speaking indecipherable words; it sounded as though the girl were on the verge of hysteria. Then he heard the calming voice of Gary Bunney responding from the Fire Cache nearby.

Landa awoke his wife, and the two of them sat in the dark and gradually pieced together what was going on. When the Landas heard Bunney promise to send an armed ranger to go after a missing girl at Granite Park, Leonard jumped to the telephone and called Bunney and volunteered for the job.

"You've got too much to do already, Leonard," his superior officer said. "I'm going in myself."

Lying in bed, Landa felt bad about the decision. As many responsibilities as he had himself, he knew that Fire Control Officer Gary Bunney had more. Bunney was coordinator of the fight against several dozen fires that were already burning, some of them dangerously, and now he would be missing from his post for at least several hours. Landa told his wife that the rescue mission should have been left to him. At least he could continue to monitor the messages between the Fire Cache and Granite Park and be ready to leave on a minute's notice if his services were needed. The young couple listened to the call for the helicopter, the progress reports through the long night, the second call for a helicopter, and finally the request that the coroner be alerted in Kalispell. "The girl must be dead," Landa said aloud. To the highly sensitive teacher of English, it was no consolation that she had been killed in another ranger's territory.

∞

At last, the radio traffic quieted, and just before dawn on this busy Sunday morning, Leonard Landa dozed off to sleep. At eight o'clock, he jumped up to the sound of his alarm and began going through the motions of dressing and bathing and stuffing a few crumbs of breakfast into his mouth. By 8:10, he was going into the cramped office alongside his bedroom, still rubbing his eyes and thinking about the events of the long night, and then he heard the sound from down the lake. Somebody was hurrying along the flat stones behind the station, and Leonard Landa prided himself on being able to read these familiar clattering noises with almost perfect accuracy.

This time, he told himself that there were several people on the stones, and they were in trouble. He opened the door of his office and fell back as four youngsters in extreme states of disarray tumbled inside and began talking simultaneously. "You won't believe this," one of them said, and another was repeating, "It seems like a bad dream, but..." A young man who appeared to be the oldest in the group was shaking violently, and Landa heard him say, "Maybe I'm not making any sense, but..." and the rest of the sentence came out so fast that Landa could not understand a word.

"Wait," Landa said. "Wait!" he pointed to one of the three young men. "You talk!" he said.

With frequent disorderly interpolations from the others, the man who identified himself as Ray Noseck told Landa a rambling story about a bear coming into their camp at Trout Lake and chasing them up trees. As Noseck spoke, Landa remembered issuing a fire permit to the group the day before, but it seemed to him that someone was missing now. Yes, there had been two girls the day before, one tall and one shorter, and now there was only the tall one, shivering and shaking as the man rambled along with his story. "Wait!" Landa said once again. "Where's the other girl? "

"She's still up there," Noseck said. "The bear dragged her away."

An involuntary shudder went through the young ranger's body, and he was not absolutely sure that he was wide awake. Events shaded into events. He had gone to bed musing about the Trout Lake bear, and then he had sat up all night listening to the crackling suggestions of a deadly bear attack over the radio, and now it seemed like the whole process was about to repeat itself. "All right," Landa said, trying to pull himself together. "All right! One of you has got to go back with me so I can figure out what the situation is. You can show me where you last saw the girl. She might be OK. She might be waiting up a tree for us."

"She's not up a tree," one of the boys said.

"We'll find out," Landa said. He picked up the phone and called headquarters. "Chief ranger's office," a voice answered, and Landa explained that a girl was missing, and he was going in to Trout Lake to look for her.

"Another girl?" the man at headquarters asked.

"It looks that way," Landa answered.

"Take your rifle," the man said, "and be careful!"

Landa loaded his .300 H&H Magnum and made sure a bullet was in the chamber. Then he pointed to the two younger boys and ordered them to accompany him over the ridge. "You take the girl back home," he said to Ray Noseck, who was comforting the distraught Denise Huckle. The young couple walked to the car that had been waiting down the lakeside road for them, and Landa, Paul Dunn, and Ron Noseck rode in the Park Service pickup a half mile to the Trout Lake trailhead. They had run and walked about a quarter mile up the steep trail when Landa realized that he had forgotten the first-aid kit in all the excitement. "You go back and get it," he said to Paul Dunn, "and catch us up the trail." The 16-year-old boy, a high-school quarter miler, hurried off without complaint, and to Landa it seemed like only a few minutes before the sturdy young boy had rejoined them, the medical supplies held tightly in his hand. Soon, someone else caught up, a man on horseback who identified himself as Andy Sampson, a weekend fisherman from Kalispell. "What's going on?" Sampson asked.

"We've had bear trouble," Landa said. "I don't know just what it is, but let us go ahead of you." Landa did not want the unarmed Sampson to reach the attack scene first and confront the bear single-handedly. All the way up and over the ridge, Sampson and his horse stayed on their heels, and once, when Sampson tried to pass, Landa moved into the middle of the path to block the way. He had the clear-cut feeling that Sampson thought they were acting hysterically, delaying his fishing trip for no good reason whatever, and the two men hardly spoke as they moved in tense procession over the ridge toward Trout Lake.

Landa looked at his watch as they were beating their way through the final patch of berry bushes above the lake, and it was 10 a.m. When they reached the logjam and saw the ruins of the original camp, the ranger looked over his shoulder and watched Andy Sampson unsheathe a long ax. Landa was relieved that his unwilling companion now seemed to understand the situation. Maybe they were all acting slightly silly, and the girl would be waiting for them in a treetop perch, but maybe she would not, too, and maybe another bear had chosen this same night to kill. It would be extraordinary after fifty-seven years without a single death, Landa told himself, but it would not be impossible. "All right," he said to Paul and Ron, "what was her name again?"

"Michele," the boys said.

The party of four spread out a few feet and began walking through the brush, calling the girl's name softly. When they reached a point about fifty yards up the lakeshore, Paul Dunn pointed to the earth and said, "This is where she was."

Landa wondered if the boy could be correct. There was no sign of the girl, none whatever. The sleeping bag was gone, nor was there an indication that a sleeping bag had ever been there. "You're sure she was here?" Landa said.

"Positive," said Paul, "and the bear dragged her up that way." He pointed into the woods up the hill.

Slowly, the four searchers worked their way up the bank and into the shadowy woods, with Landa and his cocked rifle in the lead. When they crossed the trail, the ranger's eye was caught by a patch of white lying on the path, and almost without thinking, he leaned over and picked it up. It felt like a piece of human flesh, and he took a closer look and realized that he was holding an ear. The realization came as a shock, and Landa said to himself that a human ear does not look like a human ear when it is detached from the body. There was no blood and no raggedness to the edge; it was as though the ear had been dissected neatly in a laboratory. All at once, Landa felt sick. "Here's her ear!" he blurted out, but the two boys and Andy Sampson remained calm outwardly, and the little party of searchers resumed its slow walk up the hill.

They had gone only a few feet farther when they came across the remains of the girl's sleeping bag, and from there up the slope, a trail of feathers marked the direction of the bear's travel. The searchers found themselves walking under spruce trees festooned with mosses and lichens. The ground was springy and thick with needles, and the trail went directly over several downed tree trunks spiked with jagged branches. Soon they came to a blue lightweight poplin jacket decorated with flowers, and a lightweight blouse; both were soaked with blood. Landa was studying the two articles of apparel when one of the boys called down, "Here she is! "

The ranger dropped the clothing and rushed up the hillside, almost tripping over two large logs before coming to a depression in the earth that marked where grizzlies or humans or both had once buried food and garbage. The sky was almost shut out by a canopy of spruce trees; there was squaw-hair lichen, "grizzly hair," everywhere, and some of the trees were losing their purchase in the thin soil and beginning to angle down toward the earth, mingling their upper branches with the tops of thimbleberry and mountain-ash bushes. Inexplicably, Landa found himself thinking how peaceful the scene was, and then he reached the boys' side and looked down at the remains of Michele Koons. The girl was on her back and mutilated beyond recognition. Landa could hardly tell that she was a female; her stomach and abdomen were gone, the hair missing from her head. The ranger covered his face with his hands and backed down the hill into the approaching Andy Sampson. "Don't leave the two boys up there alone!" the fisherman said, but Landa's face was pale, and it took him a few minutes to pull himself together.

∞

The Kleins, geologist Robert and schoolteacher Janet, had slept on the floor of the chalet dining room, along with eight or ten others, and when they awoke Sunday morning, they felt as though they had been up all night. With Don Gullett and one or two others, the fatigued couple hiked down to the trail cabin to pick up the equipment they had left behind, and because they were so close, they walked the 150 or 200 yards to the place where the boy and girl had camped. They retrieved the couple's knapsack and a few other small items, then retraced the harrowing journey of the night before, down the trail of bloody glacier lilies and false hellebores to the place where the bear had dropped the girl. By daylight, the trail was plain, and next to the flattened bloody spot where Julie Helgeson had lain alone and wounded, they found a Hershey bar wrapper and a full package of Lifesavers. Perhaps they had fallen out of the girl's pocket when the bear dropped her. Someone said that Julie's watch was missing, but a short search of the area did not locate the watch, if indeed it was missing in the first place.

When the expedition returned to the chalet shortly before nine, people were getting up slowly, and the few who had slept through the night were learning, to their amazement, what they had missed. Robert Klein stood on a cleared area in front of the chalet, still trying to assimilate all that had happened, and he recognized one of the three medical men, Dr. Olgierd Lindan, approaching. Lindan looked drawn and haggard, and to Robert Klein it appeared that the internist from Ohio and points east was suffering from more than tiredness. "What is it?" Klein said to the softer spoken Lindan. "What's the matter?"

"Nothing," Dr. Lindan said. "I suppose I'm just realizing what happened."

Klein lowered his voice. "Doctor," he said, "do you think the difference was that we didn't go and get her right away?"

Lindan was quiet. Then he said, "After it's all over, you always think you could have done something different."

"Would she have lived if we had gone straight after her?"

"Maybe she would," Lindan said in a voice barely audible to the man standing next to him. "At least she wouldn't have bled so much." The doctor moved away, and Klein thought that he had never seen a man appear more depressed. The realization surprised him. He had always thought that doctors were cold and unemotional, and it pleased him, as much as anything could please him on this dismal morning, to meet one who acted warm, human and sensitive.

Loud voices caught the young geologist's ear, and he turned to see two men having a brisk conversation. Klein recognized them as the same pair who had set themselves up as the resident experts on birds. While he had not wanted to start an argument, he had wanted several times the evening before to tell them that they were making some very serious misidentifications. Klein listened.

"Stupid, dumb kids, that's all they were!"

"Absolutely right! They shouldn't have been out there in the first place, but you can't tell kids nowadays."

"Inexperienced kids, they didn't know what the hell they were doing."

"And now they'll come in and kill all the bears, all on accounts of a couple of dumb kids."

Klein realized that but for a minor difference of a few hundred yards, he and his wife might have been the victims of the grizzly and might now be the object of the two bird watchers' eulogistic scorn, and when one of the men wandered over near him, Klein said, "I heard what you were saying. Don't you realize that this bear killed a human being?"

The man said, "It was the kids' own fault. Why blame the bears? They shouldn't shoot a single bear because of a couple of inexperienced, dumb kids. Those kids shouldn't even have been here."

It had been a long, difficult night, and Robert Klein, normally the least contentious of men, felt his gorge rise. "Listen," he said sharply, "those kids had just as much right to be here as you do. What the hell are you doing here anyway?"

"We came to see the bears," the man muttered.

Klein laughed. "You came to see the bears?" He affected a look of massive incredulity. "You mean to say you hiked all the way out here to stand on a porch and watch bears eat garbage?" He walked away with the air of a man who could not believe his ears, but only a few minutes later, he saw that the victim of his angry tongue had not been chastened. The man was still buttonholing people and asking them to support his plea that the grizzlies be spared. Klein shook his head and wondered about mankind.

Back inside, the process of feeding about seventy people was going slowly, and plainly the plan to leave at 9 a.m. was not going to work out. It was close to 11 when Tom Walton walked into the dining room and rapped on the side of a glass for attention. The Kleins and the others listened attentively as the young chalet keeper said, "I'm sorry about what happened. It was a tragic thing, and I appreciate all that you did. You're nice people. I don't know what to do about charging you. Some of you didn't even sleep in your beds. I talked to my boss, and he said, 'Tell them to pay what they think they should pay.' God knows it was an awful experience, and if you don't want to pay anything, don't feel guilty." A line formed at the desk, and it appeared that most of the guests were going to pay the full amount.

∞

Joan Devereaux did not know how long she had slept, but she suspected that it had not totaled more than a few minutes. Each time she had dozed off, she had found herself rounding a bend on a lonely mountain path and coming face to face with a charging grizzly. Under the circumstances, she preferred lying awake and staring at the black ceiling.

By nine, she was radioing headquarters about her plan to take the group down the Alder Trail, five miles of fairly easy path. The conversation went on for several minutes, and the young ranger-naturalist began to sense a reluctance on the part of headquarters to make a decision. After she explained her reasons for selecting the Alder Trail—it was fast and easy and most of the people were overwrought and tired and needed to get away from the chalet as quickly as possible—she waited for someone to tell her she was right or wrong, but instead she was told to stand by. Then she heard someone she recognized as Francis Elmore, the park's chief naturalist. "Four of us are coming up the Loop Trail," Elmore was telling somebody on the radio, "and I think she should take them out that way."

Joan Devereaux was glad to hear that more help was on the way, but it did not make sense to her to steer the distraught party down the Loop Trail. To be sure, it was the shortest way out to the blacktop, four miles of steep, rocky path hemmed in by berry bushes, but it was also the most precipitous, and there were several elderly people in the group who surely would have difficulty negotiating it. Also, a trip down the Loop Trail would take the party near the campground site where the attack had been made; Joan wondered how some of the hikers would react to *that* news. At first, she told herself that very few of the chalet guests knew the exact location of the attack, but this notion was canceled when a small boy pointed down to the campground and said, "Mommy, that's where the bear killed the girl, isn't it?" And as if all these reasons did not dictate staying off the Loop Trail, there was one even more important. Joan was only in her second year in Glacier Park, but along with all the other naturalists, she knew that the Loop Trail was popular with grizzlies. She had talked to some of the older guests, trying to calm their fears about being attacked on the way out, and she knew that the sight of a single bear would have sent some of them into stumbling flights of panic. The young naturalist did not want to be around when that happened.

On the other hand, she was still an Army officer's daughter, and the discipline that had enabled her to take charge the night before enabled her to take charge once again. Orders were orders, and if Francis Elmore dictated that they take the Loop Trail, there must be good and sufficient reason, regardless of her own personal fears. At least they would have the advantage of knowing that someone would be meeting them on the way out. The mere sight of an incoming party in ranger green would be good for morale.

By 10:45, the last guest had been fed, and Joan asked those who were going with her to assemble at the back of the chalet and count off. The count reached fifty-nine, but Riley Johnson, the backpacking father who had been so helpful on the rescue missions the night before, corrected it. "I counted the baby, but I didn't count myself," he said. That made sixty. Another five or six, including Father Connolly and Steve Pierre, were going out by different routes.

The mass exodus had hardly begun before the hikers encountered four men coming up the trail toward them. Three were carrying rifles; Joan recognized the fourth as the gray-haired Elmore, breathing hard but staying abreast of his juniors. Before anyone else could speak, two men in the departing group ran up to the four newcomers and begged them not to hurt the bears. "They were only acting naturally," one of the men said. "It was the kids that were at fault."

The park officials brushed by without comment and disappeared up the trail, and the others continued their long downhill hike under a relentless summer sun. At first, the trail ran through a semi-wooded area, where marmots bounced their shrill whistles off the boulders and ground squirrels stuck their heads out and suddenly disappeared behind glacier lilies without any apparent motion. Joan recognized the telltale

"Before we do anything else, we've got to clear the area," Landa said. "There're some people up at Arrow Lake."

The two strong young men headed north on the heavily wooded trail, hunting for the killer bear as they walked. At Arrow Lake, they found six hikers: four young park employees and a father and son from Roseburg, Oregon. The father and son were the same two people who had been treed the day before, but they had not let the two-hour wait in the branches interfere with their vacation, and they were busily fishing when Gildart and Landa came rushing up. "Grizzly trouble!" Gildart said. "You'll have to leave with us."

Landa found the four park employees and gave them the same message, but the two young men wanted to stay. "You can't stay," Landa said. "Now please pack your things, and let's go."

When neither of the young men made a move and one of them gave him a look of disbelief, Landa said simply, "Look, a grizzly killed a girl downtrail last night." The two girls began throwing equipment into packs, and the two men rushed to strip their camping gear, and within a few minutes, the armed party, with a ranger at front and rear, was moving back down the trail toward Trout Lake. It was a slow trip; the two girls alternately verged on hysteria and collapse. At 6 p.m., Gildart and Landa phoned headquarters from the Lake McDonald Ranger Station and reported that the area had been cleared. They were told to get a good night's sleep and report to headquarters the next morning.

∞

About an hour after they passed the motley group of hikers headed down the Loop Trail, the search-and-destroy mission of four Park Service personnel reached Granite Park Chalet in a state of puzzlement. On the last part of the three-hour uphill hike, they had begun hearing fragments of radio messages over their portable pack set. There were some cryptic remarks about bears, another request for a helicopter, some instructions about carrying rifles, and finally a short crackling message consisting of three letters: "DOA."

"It sounds like another bear attack!" one of the men said, but this made no sense, and finally they decided that they were allowing their imaginations to run rampant.

Each of the four men had his own attitude about grizzlies and his own attitude about the assignment ahead, which was to kill every grizzly that frequented the Granite Park area. Francis Elmore, the chief naturalist, was relieved that his part of the mission would consist only of tape-recording the reports of survivors and measuring distances and describing the various venues of the attack. He would function, in other words, as a sort of wildlife detective. The other three carried high-powered rifles, and there was no doubt in any of their minds that they were to use them. Robert Wasem, an experienced park biologist, was more or less in charge of the killing group, and the assignment did not sit comfortably on him. A mild, soft-spoken Ohioan, Wasem had the dedicated biologist's inevitable tendency to think of the park as a closed receptacle full of life forms that must be allowed to live as normally as possible. In such a setting, man could be the only disruptive influence. Although Wasem had hunted grouse a few times, he did not enjoy killing. He preferred to bag his wild game through the end of a spotting scope.

Cliff Martinka, originally from Pennsylvania, was a newly hired research biologist; he had just completed two and a half years with the Montana Fish and Game Department and had come to his new post in Glacier Park two weeks before. In his own way, Martinka was as dedicated a scientist as Wasem. He was so steeped in the jargon of biology (he had both bachelor's and master's degrees) that he was sometimes difficult for the layman to follow. In the world of Cliff Martinka, animals did not eat berries; "they utilized them for consumptive purposes." Bears were not killed; they were "dispatched," "taken care of," or "eliminated." Nor did Cliff Martinka have any compunction about dispatching or taking care of or eliminating bears, provided, of course, that there was no alternative. As he later explained, "I've been a hunter all my life. I've killed more than my share. Regardless of the situation, it doesn't disturb me at all to see something dead or to have to kill it. I was thinking as we climbed up there that this was something that had to be done, and if it had to be done, I preferred to be involved. I felt competent enough with a rifle, and perhaps other less experienced people may not have been able to handle the situation."

The fourth member of the execution team was a seasonal ranger and wintertime high-school teacher named Kerel Hagen, a short, wiry Montanan who had worked his way up to a high rating on the park's personnel charts despite his part-time employment. The word had gone out many summers earlier that Kerel Hagen was uniquely adaptable to the special problems of the park's backcountry, and whenever the rangers needed a wilderness troubleshooter, they tried to get him. Still in his 30s, Hagen was able to hike nonstop from one end of the park to the other, and he handled horses and rifles like a typical Montanan.

The four men arrived at the chalet just before noon and sat down for a quick lunch. The atmosphere was uneasy in the big stone-and-log building; usually there were dozens of giddy dudes milling around and occupying every space at the tables, but now there was only the chalet staff. Some of the girls had reddened eyes and disappeared around corners, sniffling, and even the ones who were not on the verge of tears looked miserable and afraid. The young innkeeper, Tom Walton, joined the newcomers and confided, "I hate to do it, but I've had to be a little tough on them. One of them keeps walking around crying and saying, 'Keep a stiff upper lip.' I told her to knock it off. She was just upsetting everybody else. Then another one said, 'We're gonna march right out of here. We can't stand it any more. This is a house of death.' Even my wife and Gracie Lundgren were acting spooky. I had to give 'em hell to straighten 'em out."

Wasem asked Walton to describe the bear situation around the chalet, and the young man from Idaho said that so far as he knew there were only two bears: a big silvertip that came around nine or nine thirty at night, and a smaller brownish bear that arrived later and chased the silvertip away. The rangers told Walton that both bears would have to be killed, and Walton said that he had expected as much, and he hoped that the girls in the chalet would be able to control themselves during the executions; some of them had become attached to the big animals.

While Francis Elmore went to work with his measuring tapes, his camera, and his recorder, the other three men took their rifles and reconnoitered the area around the chalet. For several hours, they saw nothing out of the ordinary, but at about four o'clock, a dark silvertip grizzly and a single cub were picked up in the binoculars at a range of almost two miles. The bears were feeding on berries near a small lake southeast of the chalet, and there was no reason to suspect that they were among the scavenging bears that came to the garbage dump nightly. Tom Walton took a look, and he said that he had never seen this pair before. The hunters glassed the animals off and on until 6:30, when they disappeared into the scrub.

By 8:30 that night, the three hunters were staked out under the clotheslines behind the chalet, waiting for bear No. 1. The garbage dump had been baited with a gallon glob of bread dough, laced with a half pound of bacon. Tom Walton and Ross Luding stood by with powerful flashlights, and several times they focused the beams on the dump so that the hunters could twist their scopes in. The range was about fifty yards; the men had comfortable shooting stances in canvas chairs, and no one doubted what was going to happen to each bear that appeared. From up above on the rear balcony, several of the chalet employees watched, and now and then the rangers would have to tell them to quiet down; they did not want to risk the slightest possibility of frightening away the "regular" bears.

Shortly after nine, someone came running out the back door with the news that the aggressive smaller bear, No. 2, was down at the bottom of the draw that led from Granite Park campground and appeared headed up to the dump. Minutes passed, and the rangers pushed their safeties off and on nervously, but no bear arrived. "What do you think happened?" Wasem asked Walton.

"Nothing," the innkeeper replied. "They'll be in. Just wait."

By now it was dark, except for a slight glow from a quarter moon tinted yellow-orange by a thin film of smoke from distant fires. A light breeze was blowing, and the temperature already was tumbling down toward the low fifties and forties, where it customarily spent the night. The men sat quietly, their rifles in their laps, and Walton and Luding kept reassuring them that sooner or later the bears would be in. At a few minutes after ten, a large silhouette lumbered into the gully and began scrambling up toward the dump. Instantly, Walton and Luding caught the animal in their big flashlights and were surprised to see that it was not the small grizzly, No. 2, but the beautiful silvertip, No. 1. Wasem whispered, "One. Two. Three!" and each man fired. The bear staggered and fell to the ground, and another volley of bullets slammed into its body. The animal thrashed about for a few seconds and lay still, its eyes gleaming like bright red reflectors into the direct beams of the flashlights. From the balcony above, a young girl began to sob violently.

About fifteen minutes later, the firing squad could hear a snorting sound from below the dump, and Walton whispered, "That'll be No. 2." When they were sure that the animal had reached the bread dough, Walton and Luding switched on their high beams and caught the smaller bear in a cross pattern. The animal looked up briefly and resumed its eating; performing in the glow of spotlights was not a new experience. This time, Hagen barked out the count; on "two" the bear looked up again, and on "three" the rifles sounded, and the animal catapulted into the air and came down heavily. The three men fired again, and now both bears lay side by side in death.

"That's it?" Wasem asked.

"That's it," Walton said, and the men ran across the ravine. They found that bear No. I was a female of about 350 pounds; No. 2 was also a female, but it weighed about 100 pounds less than the silvertip. Martinka and Wasem poked flashlights into the bears' mouths and spread their claws, looking for signs of guilt, but there was not so much as a speck of flesh or blood on either of them. The biologists opened the stomachs and looked for human hair or strips of cloth or skin, but all that was visible were the half-digested remains of leaves and berries and the ends of tapeworms that reached down into the intestines. The team took dozens of flash pictures and then returned to the chalet to report their kills to headquarters, and everyone was asleep by 11 o'clock. It was not long afterward that newspapers and the wire services received the word from headquarters: The killer bear of Granite Park was dead. Or was it?

Some time before, Seasonal Ranger Bert Gildart had executed a troublesome bear on instructions of his superiors, and he had no doubt about the reason he was to report to headquarters again on Monday, or why Leonard Landa was to be his partner. Presumably, Landa knew the Trout Lake area; it was part of his responsibility to patrol Trout and Arrow lakes. Gildart knew bears and guns and how to track and kill. The two of them formed the logical assassination squad for the Trout Lake bear, so they showed up at headquarters at 8 a.m. Monday, August 14, fully armed. This time, Gildart had remembered to bring his own rifle, a .30-06 converted 1903 Springfield, and he had strapped a single-action .357 Magnum Ruger revolver to his waist.

The two young rangers checked in with the chief ranger's office and waited for instructions. At 9 a.m., they were still waiting. By now, all available ranger executives had arrived, and they kept walking back and forth past Gildart and Landa at high speed, saying nothing, but appearing to be in a hurry. After a while, Gildart intercepted a high-ranking ranger and asked if they should not be heading toward Trout Lake to eliminate the killer bear. "We're seeing about that," the executive said.

Now it was 10 a.m. The two eager young men had been curbing their impatience for two hours, and still no one was paying any attention to them. The pace in the handsome new headquarters building had become more frenetic; high officials dashed in and out of the offices of higher officials and vice versa. Telephones jangled, and secretaries raced up and down the long hall to whisper in their bosses' ears. Gildart and Landa began to get the impression that no concrete steps would be taken until ordered by someone outside the park headquarters, perhaps someone as far away as the Department of the Interior building in Washington, D.C. Once again, they collared a ranger official, and once again they were told to wait. It was after 11 when they were finally instructed to hike into Trout and Arrow lakes by way of the Lake McDonald Trail and to kill every grizzly bear they encountered.

The two young men ran out of the headquarters building and almost bowled over a newspaper photographer. "Wait a minute!" the man said. "I want to get a picture of you with your guns." The two rangers brushed past without slowing stride, got into their pickup truck already loaded with camping gear and canned salmon, and roared down the blacktop toward the Trout Lake trailhead. They were on the way over Howe Ridge by noon, moving slowly and methodically, studying the terrain. Now that they were started, there was no hurry; their orders specified killing any grizzlies they encountered, and they were to stay until the area was completely clear of the big animals or until the killer bear was executed and positively identified. Sometimes they made wide detours to specific vantage points, but after four hours of silent stalking and glassing every square inch of visible territory, they had seen neither grizzly nor sign. It was 4 p.m. before they dropped down into the Trout Lake area and found their first bear scat. It was still fresh, and in the middle of it was a tiny white bone. Gildart took a closer look and saw that the bone was from a small mammal, perhaps a ground squirrel or a chipmunk.

The two hunters poked holes in several cans of salmon and walked around the logjam campsite, distributing the aromatic juice on the ground. Then they spread bits of the delicacy around the fire grate and the open beach where the hot sun could do its work. Within an hour or so, the place had begun to smell like a cannery, and Gildart and Landa waited expectantly for the bear to come out of the underbrush as it had so many times before. But when the grizzly did not appear after several hours, Landa suggested that it might make more sense to search around the area, returning from time to time to the logjam campsite to see if the bear had shown up, and thus the two men occupied themselves until early evening. When the sun dropped behind Rogers Peak, they decided that the bear might have moved uptrail toward Arrow Lake, and since they intended to camp at the Arrow Lake shelter cabin that night, they began a slow hunt toward the north, always staying near the trail that ran narrow and tortuously through high walls of berry bushes and trees. They had gone about a mile up Trout Lake when they began to notice fresh bear tracks and scats at almost regular intervals, but they had mistimed their departure, and all at once, night closed down on them. There could be no more hunting in the darkness; they were hit with the chilling realization that they had inadvertently switched roles with the killer bear, and now they had to get to the shelter cabin as quickly as possible. There was no doubt in their minds that the bear had fled in this same direction, and no doubt that it would attack human beings, and the two young rangers broke into a jog, stumbling into bushes and stopping occasionally to probe for the lost trail with their flashlights. Once Landa said breathlessly, "What was that?"

Gildart stopped, and both men heard a rustling noise in the bushes alongside. "I think it's a squirrel," Gildart said, "but let's not wait to find out."

The shelter cabin was empty; the trail had been closed by order of the park superintendent, and the two men had the 20-by-10-foot cabin all to themselves. They brought in a supply of water from the stream just down the bank, one of them doing the carrying while the other stood guard with a rifle, and after a short snack and a radio report to headquarters describing their futile day, the two men went to sleep.

∞

Shortly after dawn on Monday, biologist Cliff Martinka was studying the carcasses of the two bears at Granite Park when he realized that the bread dough and bacon strips were gone from the dump. At first, he thought that there must be thousands of hungry ground squirrels and other small mammals around the area, but he discarded the idea almost as quickly as it came to him. Only a big animal could have done away with so much food in just a few nighttime hours. Once again, he asked Tom Walton if there were any other bears that came to the garbage dump, and once again Walton said that there were no others. Earlier, when there had been snow on the ground, the tracks of an adult bear with two cubs had been seen often, but Walton said that there had been no trace of this bear family for several weeks.

The rangers pondered the matter all morning long as they busied themselves making measurements, taking more pictures of the dead bears, and patrolling the environs of the cha-

let for other grizzlies. Shortly after 2 p.m., the tall, red-haired
Dave Shea came up the trail, carrying a rifle. He was listed
on the park records as Wasem's assistant, and headquarters
had ordered him to interrupt an elk research project on the
Belly River and join his boss at Granite Park. When the young
seasonal ranger-biologist saw the two bear carcasses lying
behind the chalet, he said, "Where are the other ones?"

"What other ones?" Wasem asked.

"There's a sow with two cubs that comes late at night," Shea
said. "Bert Gildart and I saw them here last week."

Martinka and Wasem exchanged meaningful glances, and
after dinner, the firing squad, now augmented by Shea, again
took up its position behind the chalet. There was no garbage
at the dump, but the bodies of the two dead bears lay redo-
lent in the moonlight, and now and then Luding and Walton
poked their light beams to see if anything had begun to gnaw
at them. Nine o'clock passed, and 10, but Dave Shea said the
sow and cubs had not arrived until nearly midnight the week
before, and if they came at all, it probably would be an hour
or so later. A few of the hunters went to bed and left instructions that they be called at the first sign of the bears. At 10:30,
a woofing sound came from the draw below the chalet, and
the alarm went out to awaken the riflemen. For a few seconds,
cubs could be heard squealing, but then the squealing turned
into bawling and the bawling into the woofing grunts that grizzlies make when they are ready to fight. Standing at ground
level in the back of the chalet, Tom Walton said to himself
that he had never heard a bear sound so ferocious, and he
commented to Luding that the animal must have caught the
scent of the two carcasses at the dump. Just then, he heard
a noise behind him and turned to see Kerel Hagen lying in
a heap at the foot of the stairs, clutching his ankle. "I think
I've sprained it," Hagen said. "I missed the last three steps in
the dark." Out in the draw, the woofing and bawling sounds
continued, but now they were plainly moving away.

With Hagen rubbing his ankle gingerly, the hunting party discussed the situation and decided to take up watches from the balcony above to avoid spooking the wary animals again. By now, it was clear why Walton and the chalet employees had never seen the sow and cubs; the slightest sound would send them racing back down the draw. Unlike bear No. 1 and bear No. 2, these were not circus performers willing to eat in a puddle of light as dozens cheered. They were wild bears.

Shortly after midnight, Shea and Walton were alone on the balcony when they heard another woof from the draw. But before they could even alert the other men, someone in search of a midnight snack ignited a lantern in the downstairs part of the chalet, and with the first glimmer of new light, the bears once again dashed away. "Well, that's that," Walton said, preparing to go to bed. "They'll never come back a third time." Shea remained on watch.

Just before 1 a.m., Shea thought he heard a shuffling sound coming from the path that led from the trail cabin to the chalet. He strained to hear and made out a low cough; instantly, he slipped back inside the chalet to awaken the crew. Within a few seconds, Elmore and Luding were manning flashlights at the corners of the balcony, and all four riflemen were sighted in on the little circle of bare earth that marked the dim outline of the garbage dump. For a few minutes, there was no sound except the breathing of the men. Then a large shadowy form began to infiltrate its way across the open gully between the chalet and the dump, and Elmore and Wasem flipped on their lights. They picked up the outline of a medium-sized grizzly about five feet from the dump, and Hagen snapped, "One! two! three!" and all the guns sounded together. The bear spun around wildly and began to bawl at the cubs, but the lights stayed sharply on the adult bear, and another volley sent it sprawling and flopping to the ground. It was exactly forty-eight hours and five minutes since the attack on Julie Helgeson.

In all, eleven shots had been fired, but only one by Dave

Shea. On the first round, the scope of his rifle had kicked into his eye and cut it open, and now a thin stream of blood ran down to his chin. When the last reverberation had come back from the surrounding mountains and died away, another sound could be heard from the hillside above the dump. The two cubs were running away, whimpering and bawling, and after a few minutes, they were hidden in the rock cover.

Everyone in the hunting party, including the bloodied Shea and the limping Hagen, rushed across the ravine to inspect the latest kill. Martinka dropped to his knees and examined the bear's paws. There was a reddish substance that looked to be blood matted in the hairy spaces between claws. A pad hung loose from one of the hind paws like a flapping half sole, and the biologist realized that the old injury must have kept the bear in constant pain. Quickly, he ran the salient facts through his brain: The bear apparently was in the habit of coming to the dump after the chalet had closed for the night, at about the same time that Julie Helgeson had been killed; the bear was a sow with cubs, and this was the most volatile kind of grizzly; the bear's ripped foot would have kept it in an angry mood; and the bear was bloodstained. Kneeling alongside the carcass, Martinka looked up at the others and said, "We got her. This is the one." Wasem cut into the stomach and found undigested bread dough, and pictures were snapped and measurements taken, and gradually the participants in the midnight execution became of a single mind about the grizzly. Twenty-four hours after the word had gone out that the killer bear was dead, the killer bear *was* dead.

∞

Gildart was up at 4 a.m., and he shook Landa. Both men peeked through the door of the shelter cabin into the black night. They agreed that there was nothing to be done until daylight, and for two hours they lay on their cots refining their hunting plans for the day. Just before 6, Gildart opened the door of the cabin and took a few paces toward the stream that ran just in front, and out of the shadows to his right he thought he detected movement. The young ranger stopped and turned his head slowly toward the north. At first, he could see nothing; night and day were still a blend, and visibility was slight. But as he peered toward a bend in the trail about thirty or forty feet away, he made out what appeared to be an expanse of fur, and then a grizzly bear, humped and unmistakable, padded out of the brush toward him. Gildart spun around and saw that it was about ten feet to the open door of the cabin. He thought he could make it to safety if the grizzly charged, and he patted his holster and felt the .357 Magnum, hoping all the time that the animal would stop, because a bear with pistol slugs in it was likely to be more dangerous than a bear in good health. There was no movement of air and no sound whatever, and only a second or two passed before Gildart realized that the grizzly was not going to stop. "Bring the rifles out!" he shouted to Landa. "Here's the bear! "

At the sound of the human voice, the animal halted, made a few shuffling movements with its front feet as though it were going to continue, then slipped sideways into the thick brush that grew like African jungle along the steep banks of Camas Creek. As he heard Landa rushing around in the cabin, Gildart took careful note that the grizzly had not backed up, not an inch, but only sidestepped into the heavy canopy of bushes. Gildart reminded himself that he and Landa were there to kill grizzlies, not just to protect their own lives, and he realized that the bear's actions suggested three possibilities: that the animal was crossing the creek and running up the slope on the opposite side; that the bear was using the cover of the stream banks to beat a retreat upstream, or that the bear was proceeding downstream, in which case it would have to pass about twenty five feet in front of the shelter cabin. A normal bear would have taken either of the first two routes, but then Gildart was not certain that he was dealing with a normal bear.

Landa thrust the .30-06 into Gildart's hands and said, "You're not kidding around, are you?"

"No," Gildart said. "There's a bear right out there."

The two men stood side by side facing the place where the stream bank dropped off six or eight feet straight down. If the bear was going to attack them, it would have to come from that direction. The light remained as grainy as ever. Neither man spoke, and there was not a sound, not even the rustle of a leaf. The busy stream seemed muted. Two or three minutes passed, and then Gildart said softly, "There he is!"

Landa squinted into the half-light, saw the grizzly, and said with awe, "Look at that head!"

The bear had worked its way downstream till it was underneath the bank directly in front of the shelter cabin, and now it was looking over the edge of the bank, reconnoitering the area, turning its head slowly from side to side as though trying to pick up a scent in the dead air. Once, the dark animal seemed to be trying to brace itself for a push up and over the bank, but then the head and shoulders slipped back out of sight, and Landa said, "Let's don't let him get away!"

Seconds passed, and inch by inch the head began to rise again above the bank. When its eyes were in sight, the bear made a sudden upward thrust that exposed its neck and shoulders, and Gildart took a step forward to shorten the range. At this motion, the bear slipped quickly from sight again, and Gildart backed off. More seconds passed, and then the bear was in violent motion, hauling itself up and over the bank to charge. In the sights of his gun, Gildart could see nothing but a great expanse of furry neck and chest, and he fired at a range of less than twenty feet. Almost in the same split second, Landa's .300 H&H Magnum went off, and the bear did a giant back dive and fell heavily into the bottom of the gulch. Gildart rushed across the clearing toward the stream, and Landa shouted, "Take it easy! This is the most dangerous time!" but Gildart was already scrambling down the bank of Camas Creek, and Landa levered a bullet into the chamber of his rifle and followed him down. Instantly, the two experienced hunters knew that the great bear was dead; there were two jagged holes seeping blood, one in the chest and one in the head; either would have been fatal. Gildart dropped to his hands and knees and saw that the bear was a brownish-colored old sow with worn-down molars and a thin, almost scrawny body.

"Let's haul her up to the cabin," he said, but the bank was too steep and slippery, and the two rangers decided to let the animal lie where it had fallen. They discussed the idea of opening the stomach to see what they could find, but Gildart said he preferred to leave any autopsies to his superiors. After they had radioed headquarters that they had killed a bear, the two friends sat in the little shelter cabin and wondered whether they had shot the right grizzly. Gildart said he was sure they had.

"What makes you so sure?" Landa asked.

"Well, what do you think she was doing around the cabin this morning?" Gildart said. "She was stalking us. And that's not normal for a grizzly."

Landa said he had to agree that the bear had not acted normally. The two men waited for orders to call off their hunt, but when no such orders came, they wandered back down the trail toward Trout Lake to search for more grizzlies. They saw plenty of fresh sign, but no bears.

∞

The rangers at Granite Park maintained their watch through the rest of the dark hours of Tuesday morning, on the off chance that there was still another anonymous bear coming into the dump at night, but they heard nothing except the soft sighing of a light breeze and the occasional distant bawling of the cubs. Wasem drew the final shift, from 4 to 6 a.m., and he heard nothing whatever, not even a breeze. He sat in a canvas chair on the upper balcony and wondered where the cubs had gone and what would happen to them now that their mother was dead. He was thankful that no one, in the wild excitement of the shooting, had pegged a bullet at the young bears. By now, they were 8 or 9 months old and weaned to a normal diet, and there was reason to believe that they had a chance for survival.

When daylight came, the biologist walked across the ravine and up the steep side of the lava flow where the cubs had been seen last, but there was no trace of them. Wasem's shift was over, but he had been up almost all night, and he figured he might as well finish his assignment. The evening before, park headquarters had radioed that one of the most obstreperous journalists in the area, G. George Ostrom of Kalispell, would be arriving at the chalet the next morning, and a high-ranking ranger executive had ordered Wasem and the other members of the party to remove all traces of dead bears before the arrival of the press. With his bandaged assistant, Dave Shea, senior biologist Wasem started down toward the trail cabin at about 7:30 to get some rope to drag the carcasses away. The two men had gone a short distance when Shea heard a bawling noise and spotted the cubs on some rocks about 150 yards below the chalet in the draw that led to the campground. Shea turned toward the chalet and saw Cliff Martinka standing several hundred yards away. "There they are!" Shea shouted up to the other biologist and gave chase with Wasem. As they ran across the rocky ground near timberline, shots rang out. Both men looked up and saw that Martinka was taking aim for another shot at the young bears. Now the cubs seemed to double their pace and headed for the far edge of the bench and the underbrush that ran down the hill on the other side. Martinka fired a few more times, but soon the bears were gone. In the bushes not far from where Julie Helgeson had been killed, Wasem and Shea found fresh spots of blood, and they knew that one of the cubs had been wounded.

∞

When G. George Ostrom turned on the radio in his house in Kalispell and heard the news that two 19-year-old girls had been killed by grizzlies during the night, he turned to his wife and said, "My God, there goes the last grizzly in Montana!" Like a movie preview, a whole sequence of future events passed through Ostrom's mind. He could see the letters to the editor mounting up and finally reaching a fortissimo; he could hear the voices on the floor of the state legislature and all the way to Washington, demanding that Glacier National Park be made safe for the public; he could see the National Park Service bending with the public pressure, and finally he could see bands of official hunters entering the park from all corners, bearing with them .30-06 rifles and widemouthed bear traps and cyanide charges and orders to kill every last specimen of *Ursus arctos horribilis* or drive them across the border into Canada.

It was not that George Ostrom was a fanatical protector of grizzlies or any other predator. He was a hunter, an enthusiastic one, and he had shot his share of bears, including a massive grizzly when he was a young boy. But like certain members of the Park Service staff, Ostrom had a deep respect for this biggest of land carnivores and a deeper respect for nature's checks and balances. He also knew that there were times when a grizzly or two had to be exterminated in the greater interests of both bears and humans. Certainly this was one such time, and Ostrom wished that he could be whisked into the park to help do the job crisply and efficiently.

At 32, G. George Ostrom had been a smoke jumper, banker, photographer, journalist, radio announcer, advertising man, and lifelong student of bears and nature. With his black wavy hair and mustache, strident voice, earthy vocabulary, and deep sense of anger and righteousness, he was a one-man *cause celebre* around his home town of Kalispell. His prize-winning column in the prize-winning weekly, the *Hungry Horse News,* was read and discussed and praised and condemned by everyone who could read, especially by the National Park Service. For several years, Ostrom had been dissatisfied with the operation of the park that he had been visiting all his life, and his columns had made him *persona non grata* with the ranger executives. Every host in the nearby towns of Columbia Falls and Martin City and Kalispell and Whitefish knew that one either invited G. George Ostrom or the top rangers, never both. Years before, someone had invited Ostrom and two ranger executives, and when a question-and-answer session began, Ostrom stood up, announced that he was speaking in his capacity as president of the local wildlife federation, and asked the rangers, "Is it true that you allow the concessioner to feed grizzlies at Granite Park?"

The rangers said that they doubted that it was true, but they certainly would look into the matter on the earliest possible occasion.

"It's true, isn't it, that the feeding of bears is one of the most dangerous practices in the park and that it's strictly against the law?" Ostrom said.

The rangers said that he was absolutely correct and that the law was enforced impartially.

"Well, then, tell me how many people have been arrested in the last ten years for feeding bears," Ostrom said.

The rangers said they would have to check the records. Ostrom asked them for an educated guess. The rangers said that they did not deal in educated guesses, and they would have to look in the files.

Ostrom said, "Don't bother looking in the files. I've already looked in your files. In the last ten years, you've arrested nobody for feeding bears. Nobody. *Zero*. And everybody on the main street of Kalispell knows that you can see grizzlies any night of the summer by watching the garbage dump at Granite Park. Now what are you gonna do about it?"

The rangers said that they would have to check the facts, and from then on, no ranger would go to a public event if the name of G. George Ostrom was on the guest list. Ostrom did not mind. He found that the turnover of rangers and ranger officials was so rapid that hardly any of them stayed on the premises long enough to learn more than the minimum about the park that was under their stewardship; it was not like the old days when a ranger might be stationed in the park for fifteen or twenty years and one could throw him a barrage of questions and get an answer to every one. Ostrom had his own coterie of friends inside the ranger headquarters—men who did not agree with park policies but could not afford to say so out loud—and it amused him a little and frightened him a lot that when difficult questions would come up, these friends would telephone him instead of turning to their superiors. G. George Ostrom was the ex officio authority on Glacier National Park, and nobody knew it better than the top rangers.

"My God, it happened," Ostrom told his wife on the morning of August 13, "and it happened exactly the way we were afraid it would happen." He had to dial park headquarters several times before there was an answer, and then he was told that there was nothing to report.

"Well," Ostrom said, "can I hike in and see for myself what happened?"

"The trails are closed," the voice from headquarters told him.

"Even to the press?"

"Even to the press."

As the day went on, journalist Ostrom fidgeted and fumed and tried to figure out what to do. He went to the hospital in Kalispell to interview Roy Ducat, but nurses whisked him out of the room before the conversation could begin. He called headquarters again and was told that the trails were still closed to everyone, including the press. Now the radio stations around Kalispell began listing the park's various explanations and theories about the twin killings. The bears had become crazed by the 100-odd lightning strikes of two days before; the bears had been made cranky by the long hot spell; the bears had become panicky from the fires; the bears had been excited by the fact that both girls wore cosmetics; the bears were upset by a sonic boom; the bears were aggravated by tourists who threw rocks at them. No hypothesis was too wild to escape mention, and George Ostrom thought he had never heard so much buncombe in his life. One commentator reported that there was a rumor that bears had been fed at Granite Park, but the very next newscast carried the park's denial: There was a gas incinerator at the chalet, and any leftover scraps were buried. Listening to such information, Ostrom worked up a powerful head of steam.

On Monday, the press embargo continued, and Ostrom called a friend on *Life* magazine in New York and asked for a formal assignment to the case. *Life* and the Associated Press and United Press International and the *New York Times* and all news media had the same problem as Ostrom: The only information that was coming out of Glacier Park was being funneled through park headquarters, and no firsthand observers were being allowed in. Ostrom's friend on *Life* told him to consider himself assigned and wished him luck on breaking down the embargo.

Now the angry journalist rang up the park once again and identified himself as "G. George Ostrom of *Life* magazine."

"Who?" the switchboard voice said.

Ostrom said, "I'm covering for *Life,* and I want to talk to the superintendent."

By late afternoon, G. George Ostrom of *Life* had had several conversations with park officials, but nothing had changed. Just before nightfall on Tuesday, almost three full days after the attacks on the girls, he picked up the phone, dialed headquarters, and announced that he was going into the park the next morning with or without permission. The voice on the other end said the trails were closed, and Ostrom said that he was going to open them singlehandedly at dawn the next day. Within an hour, permission had been granted.

Late on Tuesday morning, a weary George Ostrom, necklaces of cameras beating on his chest, staggered up the last switchback and headed across the bench toward the Granite Park Chalet. As he approached, he recognized Ross Luding and the kitchen superintendent, Eileen Anderson, and four or five young girls, plus the execution squad of four park personnel. Immediately, one of the rangers turned to a two-way radio and began talking, and as soon as the conversation had ended, Ostrom began receiving terse instructions. The carcass of one bear was waiting to be carried out for autopsy, he was told, but the other two had been dragged down the hill and were not to be photographed. "Why not?" Ostrom asked.

"We don't want any publicity on it," one of the rangers said.

For the first of several times during that day, Ostrom lost his temper. "It's none of your business what you get publicity on and what you don't," he snapped. "This is my park as much as it's yours, and I'm taking the pictures."

As he walked down the hill to find the dead bears, he saw that the radio was in use again. "How about coming down and standing over your trophies?" Ostrom said.

"No, thanks," the bear killers told him.

He saw two men heading down the mountain with rifles, and when he asked them what they were doing, they said they were hunting the cubs. "Cubs?" Ostrom said. "Were there cubs?" He was told that there had been two, that they had been sighted earlier in the morning, and that attempts to shoot them had failed.

"You tried to shoot the cubs?" the puzzled Ostrom asked.

It was explained that the young animals would not have survived the winter, and killing them would be an act of mercy. Ostrom fought to control his temper. "Who says that cubs can't make it through the winter?" he said evenly. "I've read everything I can get my hands on about grizzly bears, and there are a lot of guys that lived their whole lives with grizzlies, and they think that a cub has a chance to make it, and two cubs together have an even better chance to make it."

One of the men said, "There was another reason. Those cubs were trained to eat at the dump. If they're not killed, they'll keep coming back to the garbage."

Ostrom stood up, unsheathed his knife, and flung it into the ground in a fit of blind rage. "God damn it!" he said. "The cubs won't come back to the garbage if *there isn't any garbage to come back to!* It's that goddamned simple!" The enraged Ostrom finally brought himself under control and said in a milder tone of voice, "I would like one of you to tell me who decided to shoot the cubs. Whose decision was that?" But no one answered.

∞

Just before noon, a helicopter arrived at Granite Park Chalet with two cases of lye. The Park Service wanted to hasten the complete eradication of the carcasses of bear No. 1 and bear No. 2 before other grizzlies were attracted by the odor. The carcass of the third bear, thought to be the killer, was stuffed into the cabin of the helicopter, and Martinka, Elmore, and Hagen climbed inside with the smelly grizzly for the return to headquarters. Later in the day, Martinka was ordered to fly into Arrow Lake and examine a bear shot by Bert Gildart and Leonard Landa. The pilot landed about a half mile away, and the young biologist had to bushwhack his way to the shelter cabin. He found the grizzly lying where it had been shot; he removed the head and paws for evidence and then took a single slice into the dead animal's stomach. Undigested matter oozed out, and in the middle of it was a ball of hair.

∞

By Wednesday morning, four days after the double killings, Bob Wasem and his assistant, Dave Shea, were the only representatives of the National Park Service at Granite Park

Chalet, and since no grizzlies had been sighted after Monday night, they decided that the mission had been accomplished. Wasem radioed the chief ranger's office, learned that the trails into the chalet were closed, and received permission to hike out via the Alder Trail to Logan Pass. Before the two biologists departed, they sprinkled fresh lye on the carcasses of the dead bears. The bawling cubs had been hanging around the corpses, and apparently they would not leave until both grizzlies had been converted into dust. At 10:15 a.m., Wasem and Shea tightened the hitches in their packs and said good-bye to the overwrought staff of the chalet. The two men had not gone far along the trail when they came to a high point, and they stopped to take a last look at the wooded valley below. "There they are!" Wasem said, pointing to a narrow stream far down the slope. The two cubs were running along the banks, and every few minutes one of them would dip its head in the water and shake it vigorously from side to side. Shea pulled out his binoculars for a better look, and he saw that part of the cub's jaw had been shot away.

"Let's go," he said to Wasem, and the two saddened biologists resumed their long walk back to civilization.

EPILOGUE

For weeks after the killings, Glacier National Park remained in a state of shock. The unthinkable had happened; the impossible had become possible, and the wondrous world of glaciers and limber pines and water shrews and wolverines and grizzlies now had new and indefinable dimensions.

People berated themselves because two innocent girls were dead. W. R. "Teet" Hammond told a friend: "I met Michele Koons and talked a little bit in the gift shop where she worked. She was a cute-looking little blond girl, and the thing you remember about her is she was so pleasant and nice to old folks like me. She died a horrible death up there, and I could have killed that bear a thousand times. *I could have killed him a thousand times.*" Characteristically, the retired New Mexico sheriff failed to mention that it was not his job to kill the bear, that it was the job of others who failed.

There were more self-recriminations about the death of Julie Helgeson at Granite Park. A member of the chalet's kitchen staff wrote her parents: "All I could think of was the girl laying there, hearing us come and building up her courage and hope and then to hear us leave without finding her. How she must have felt!"

Tom Walton spent hours going over what had happened and then going over it again. With a clear objectivity that is vouchsafed to few, he summed up his thoughts one day. "I often say to myself that we should have gone down and got the girl right away. I wish I would have. And I say to myself that I would go straight after her if I had it to do over again. We had no arms, nothing, not even a pocket knife. But you still have to wonder. If she hadn't been out there for two hours in the cold, bleeding to death...." Naturalist Joan Devereaux, winner of $250 and a National Park Service medal for her plucky behavior on the night of the attack, was one of the few who entertained no self-doubt. "I guess, in a way, I'm the reason why we didn't go charging out in the woods looking for the girl," she said, "but I didn't know what the situation was, and there was no sense in risking anybody else's life and go out there."

At ranger headquarters, the slightest mention of the case for months afterward was enough to send executives dashing from office to office for consultation, preening the files by the hour, and repeatedly dialing Washington for guidance. The press, along with the general public, was barred from the venues of the tragedies, and the facts that were hand-fed to newsmen seemed to be carefully selected by ranger officials for their irrelevance. Eventually, it was learned that the Montana Livestock Sanitary Board examined the brains of all four dead bears and reported that none was rabid and that the blood around the claws of the Granite Park bear was tested by the FBI and proven to be of non-human origin. Nor was there any other physical evidence against the old sow; like Bruno

Hauptmann, she was convicted on strong, circumstantial evidence. Days later, the FBI reported that the Trout Lake grizzly had in her stomach "65 light-brown to dark-brown head hairs of Caucasian origin ranging from 3/4 to 5 1/8 inches," leaving no doubt as to that bear's palpable guilt.

If facts were rare, theories were cheap, and the news wires hummed with them. Early in the theorizing, an official of the park had told a journalist that the 100 or so lightning strikes less than two days before the killings might have crazed the bears, and the report turned up in many newspapers.

Glen Cole, the research superintendent for the Rocky Mountain National Parks, announced, "We may have to impose more restraints on hikers. Maybe they shouldn't have been in there. You just don't take a dog into that country."

Joan Devereaux, blooded now and no longer the insecure rookie naturalist of the past, said, "We have a lot of accidents throughout the summer involving these young people. The problem is that after they've been here a week or two, they figure they know everything there is to know about everything—climbing, hiking, camping—and they just don't."

A humane society worker telephoned a high official of Glacier Park, and the details of the conversation were recorded in an office memo. The ranger official wrote:

This lady wanted to know why, after 50 years, the bears would go on a rampage in the park. Also, does the park feed the bears? She was told that the bears go to the dumps in campgrounds, are fed by people, from garbage cans. They smell the cooking of campers, find scraps, spilled food. Bears know that people mean food and they go to the area to find something to eat—are scared away for a while, but eventually become bolder and will attack to get fed. They dragged off the sleeping bags for food possibilities, occupants struggled and were killed.... She also wanted to know if it was against the law to sleep on the ground in campgrounds—was told that many people do this, all over the park. The newspapers like to make the stories sound exciting and attract attention by head-lines. The park makes no attempt to kill all bears—only the troublesome ones who cannot be discouraged from molesting humans. She wanted to know if bears change their disposition overnight and was told that the people spoil the bears by feeding them until they become bold and cannot be frightened off and they will hurt people to get food. No more bears will be shot as it seems certain that the culprits have been eliminated.

The import of such messages, flowing out of park headquarters by the dozens, was that somehow "the people" had caused the bears to attack, and "the newspapers" had blown the stories up.

Almost a year went by before the Park Service issued its own report on the incidents, and by then the facts had been so obscured that the public was ready to accept anything. The unsigned report managed to convey the impression that a combination of curious events had combined to cause the deaths of the two girls. The report admitted offhandedly that grizzlies had been known to dine on table scraps in the park and that the Trout Lake bear "had obtained food several times earlier at the same location," but these two most significant of all facts were buried under thousands of words of supposi-tion about lightning strikes, cosmetics, atmospheric pressures, menstrual cycles, availability of natural food, bear psychology, and other extraneous matters. Nowhere in the report was there the flat statement that the National Park Service had countenanced summer long feeding at Granite Park, estab-lished a campground in an area that had been frequented for decades by feeding grizzlies, and allowed a marauding bear to terrorize campers for three months.

∞

A larger question remained: After nearly six decades of relative innocence, why had *Ursus arctos horribilis* chosen a four-hour period on the morning of August 13, 1967, to kill two 19-year-old girls? Philip Youngman, curator of mammals at the National Museum of Canada, spoke for many. "It is just too much to buy the story that sheer coincidence caused two grizzly bears only twenty miles apart to attack two similar camping parties at almost the same time," he said. Immediately, a statistician began punching away on a computer and reported that the odds against one such killing on a single night were 1 million to 1; the odds against two in the same night were 1 trillion to 1. But a computer is only as accurate as the information fed into it, and the primary statistic fed into this particular computer was the fifty-seven-year record of no deaths from grizzlies. The phrase "zero out of fifty-seven" is arithmetically meaningless, of course, and can only lead to mathematical mischief. Had the computer been fed *all* the data, including the real data concerning the events of the summer of 1967, it would not have posted such long odds. As it was, the machine only compounded the mystery of the two attacks.

To understand the simultaneity of the incidents, it is better to begin with ancient history than modern mathematics. Man and grizzly had been on a collision course for tens of thousands of years. At the precise second when the first man stepped onto the North American plains and the first grizzly looked up from his grazing to try to catch the scent of the pale, upright intruder, the biological alarm clocks had been set. But why did two of them go off on a single night eons later? There seem to be two reasons: By 1967, man with his hated smell and his bumbling manner was pushing harder and harder on the grizzly, and the National Park Service chose that summer to present the annoyed and harassed bears with engraved invitations to strike. It is pure coincidence indeed that two grizzlies chose a few hours of a single night to take two victims who had much in common, but it is no coincidence at all that the year in which this happened was 1967, and the place Glacier Park.

Consider the grizzly's well-documented ways, his insular nature, his abhorrence of man. The myriad grizzlies that used to feed on the plains of Kansas and dig for pocket gophers in South Dakota and hunt berries in the front range of the Colorado Rockies took refuge in the farthest reaches of frontier Montana and Wyoming simply to get away from man, and then one day they found themselves backed into a few thousand square miles of their native land. For a few decades, the situation was tolerable, but after World War II, the great bear began to lose his freedom once again. Hikers were beginning to march at him from all directions, and the grizzly retreated farther and farther into the dark recesses of the two great parks where he was concentrated: Yellowstone and Glacier. Relief came easier in Yellowstone; it was not essentially a trail park, and there were vast areas where no human beings set foot. But as the postwar years went on, almost 1 million tourists were showing up each season at Glacier Park, and a goodly number of them were taking to the beautiful trails that led straight into the domain of the grizzly and were camping out in areas the bears had considered their own. By human standards, the percentage of people in the 1,600 square miles of the park was low. By grizzly standards, the place was as crowded as Times Square on Saturday night. A normal grizzly thinks nothing of foraging over eight or ten miles at a time, and if he sees a single human, he runs away. Now the grizzlies were seeing humans wherever they turned and seeing them again when they fled.

Habitués of Granite Park were understandably quick to claim that the feeding of bears in their backyard had nothing to do with the tragedy of Julie Helgeson, and one of them said, "Why, I can remember when there were fourteen grizzlies in a single night feeding on our table scraps, and

nobody was ever harmed." But this was in the distant past
when there were perhaps twenty or thirty guests registered
at the chalet, all of them *inside,* and it made no difference
how many grizzlies came to the dump and disappeared back
into the blackness of the wilderness. In the week that ended
so horribly on the morning of August 13, Granite Park had
been a crossroads of humanity. Longhaired girls dipped up
and down the path used by the grizzlies; hikers stumbled
up the same trail at the very time that bears were feeding
in the back of the chalet; five or six dozen people at a time
jammed elbow-to-elbow every night to watch the grizzlies
come in, and human forms in sleeping bags were to be found
all over the place. Everyone waited to see the pets, and no
one dreamed that the pets would strike. On the night of the
attacks, every available inch of space inside the chalet was
crammed with humans; several others slept in bags on the
porch; a few were to be found at various distances from the
blockhouse building; three slept several hundred yards away
at the trail cabin, and another couple was in the campground
down on the bench. And into this high-density area, grizzly
bears were being lured by table scraps with the tacit consent
of the National Park Service. No wonder that someone was
killed. At Trout Lake, the situation was only slightly different. Almost every visitor to the lake during the hot summer
of 1967 reported coming upon other humans, and this in
an area that demanded a 2,000-foot climb up and another
1,500-foot climb down, or in the alternative, a slight uphill
walk of more than seven miles along the Camas Creek drainage; Trout Lake had always been a relatively popular area,
but not so popular that day after day the campsite would be
occupied, the shoreline dotted with improvised camps, the
shelter cabin a few miles upstream completely crammed with
humans. The berry crop was lean in the fiery-hot summer
of 1967, and grizzlies had little choice but to mingle with
the numerous people at Trout Lake. There were few other

places where berries were available in quantity, and there were few other places where grizzlies could get away from people anyway. And so they tried to abide the unpleasant man smell, and out of all their numbers a single aging specimen took the process one step too far and became contemptuous of man and even came to covet the smell and flavor of the species' only living enemy.

One may argue that the rangers should have seen the problem coming, and indeed there are bits and pieces of evidence to show that they did. Still they took no action. Bears had not killed in the entire history of the park; why would anyone assume that they would kill this summer? One does not prepare for the unthinkable. If one "knows" that something will not happen and cannot happen, one may violate one's own laws accordingly, and no one will ever be the wiser. It was not necessary to enforce the rules about bear feeding at Granite Park or exterminate the rogue bear at Trout Lake; everyone knew that grizzlies did not kill humans, that "it can't happen here." This strategy, of course, was valid only so long as the grizzlies continually fled before man. But no powerful carnivore, least of all the proudly independent grizzly, will go gently into the dark night of extinction. At some point, a stand must be made, and in 1967, for a multiplicity of reasons, the grizzlies were finally making it.

Aside from their miscalculations about what the grizzly would and would not do, there was another reason why the dedicated and sincere rangers of Glacier National Park failed to take action when action was so clearly demanded. F. Scott Fitzgerald said, "Show me a hero and I will write you a tragedy." To the men in the green uniforms of the National Park Service, the grizzly was a hero, the subconscious symbol of the vanishing frontier, the last of the big, footloose omnivores of the American West. Such heroes carry within themselves the stuff of tragedy; people break rules for them, make concessions to them, turn the other cheek to them, until sometimes the heroes wind up destroying themselves. Grizzlies had never killed in the park; therefore they never *would* kill in the park. It was easy for the rangers to accept such a proposition, especially since it coincided with their inner tendency to think only the grandest thoughts about the heroic grizzly. Generations of naturalists have felt and acted the same.

∞

Two weeks after the killings in Glacier Park, a grizzly chewed off his keeper's arm in the Milwaukee County Zoo. A month later, a hunter named Bert Bell, of Cody, Wyoming, was badly lacerated by a wounded grizzly that was not strong enough to push the attack to a conclusion. The rangers in Glacier Park read about these incidents and worried. As Chief Ranger Ruben Hart said, "For fifty-seven years, no one was ever killed or seriously injured here, and suddenly in one night it happens twice. Then you're on the spot from that point on."

Less than three months went by before the next attack in the region of Glacier Park. A burly 47-year-old Californian named Robert Gilmore was hunting in the North Fork of the Flathead River just outside the park boundaries when a male grizzly jumped him and inflicted deep cuts on his face and head. The bear was still clawing and chewing on Gilmore when his hunting companions dispatched the animal with eight shots.

The next spring, a schoolteacher-naturalist named Robert Hahn was on a one-man hike near Siyeh Creek in Glacier Park when he spotted a grizzly sow and her cub at a range of several hundred yards. The 30-year-old amateur photographer began filming the animals with a telescopic "zoom" lens, and he became so engrossed in his work that he failed to realize that the bears were coming dangerously close. They were, in fact, only 65 feet away when Hahn stood up to signal his presence. The cub retreated, but the sow charged instantly. Hahn had barely started up a tree 15 feet away when the bear's jaws gripped his leg and wrenched him to the ground. The embankment was steep and covered with snow, and the two combatants rolled and tumbled 200 feet down the slope before Hahn grabbed another tree and tried to climb out of the enraged sow's range. This time, the mother bear scrambled 20 feet up the tree after him and nipped at his feet and legs before falling to the ground and disappearing in the brush.

Hahn recovered without difficulty at Cardston Hospital across the international border in Canada, and from his bed, he issued a request that the two bears not be hunted down and destroyed. "It was my fault," he said. "I was intruding in her territory, and I had no right to be there." Glacier Park officials closed the trail for a week, found no sign of the two grizzlies, and reopened it. But despite the relatively happy ending to the story of this attack, ranger executives were shaken to their boot tops. The killings of the year before could no longer be viewed as flukes, as one-in-a-trillion shots that would never happen again. Twice in the intervening months, once inside the park boundaries and once just outside, grizzlies again had committed the unthinkable.

When Glacier Park opened for the summer season of 1968, rangers and staff biologists had laid down the most rigorous system of bear control in National Park Service history. Grizzlies were placed on the strictest probation. If a bear bothered human beings more than once, it was to be shot summarily. If a grizzly was trapped, ear-tagged and removed to another area, and then returned on its own to the point of its first capture, it was shot. Rangers had the authority to kill instantly any bear, black or grizzly, that showed aggressive tendencies near developed areas. When a grizzly tore the seats out of a car parked near Kintla Lake, it was tracked down and killed with no further ado.

Dozens of other steps were taken. Trails were closed at the first sign of a grizzly. Campsites were shut down and reopened only when foraging grizzlies had moved away. Warning signs were posted everywhere, and information about bears was placed at every trail head. A strict "pack in, pack out" policy was initiated; hikers had to haul out their empty cans and other trash, and one ranger was placed on permanent horseback patrol throughout the park to see that the rule was obeyed. All unnatural sources of food, such as the dumps at Polebridge and Granite Park, were removed, and the Park Service's long-standing rules against feeding bears were strictly enforced for the first time in anyone's memory.

Ironically, the stern program of 1968 seemed to have a more telling effect on the park's relatively harmless black bears. Twenty black bears were put to death, or about three times the summertime average. But the grizzlies seemed to sense that a crackdown was on, and relatively few sightings were made. The only grizzlies to be executed were the one at Kintla Lake and the cub that had been wounded the year before at Granite Park. Early in 1968, the young bear was seen near Many Glacier, but it was in poor physical condition and unable to feed properly with its shattered jaw. A ranger put the pathetic creature out of its misery.

To many, these killings were insufficient. For the first time in history, a substantial body of public opinion called for the formal annihilation of *Ursus arctos horribilis* in the continental United States. To be sure, the pro-grizzly sentiment outweighed the anti-grizzly sentiment, but no one could remember a time when so many people were willing to stand up and demand that the animal be put to death. The influential *Montana Standard*, published in Butte, warned that tourist travel would fall damagingly low if the grizzlies were not eliminated. A woman from Chase, British Columbia, demanded that all grizzlies be shot on sight. "Many good people lived long useful good lives and never saw a grizzly bear in any form," she said. Forest "Nick" Carter, retired chief ranger of Glacier National Park, worked up a plan for a four-man execution squad "to do nothing but hunt and trap the grizzly." After a few years of wholesale killing, the squad would be reduced to two men on a permanent basis. Then "all trails in the park would be safe for travel of all kinds," Carter said. "The national park is for the use of the people. That means every bit of it."

Defenders of the great bear answered by quoting the National Park Service's mandate. "The animals indigenous to the parks shall be protected, restored if practicable, and their welfare in a natural wild state perpetuated." The park might be for the people, as Nick Carter kept saying, but it was also for the grizzlies and the wolverines and the martens and all the other animals that had lived within its borders for centuries. When the anti-grizzly forces argued that it would suffice for the species to survive north of the American border, the conservationists answered by quoting Aldo Leopold, who once said, "There seems to be a tacit assumption that if grizzlies survive in Canada and Alaska, that is good enough. It is not good enough for me. Relegating grizzlies to Alaska is about like relegating happiness to heaven; one may never get there."

And so the battle of words raged, not only in provincial newspapers like the *Hungry Horse News* and the *Daily Inter Lake,* but in metropolitan dailies as far removed from Glacier Park as New York and Los Angeles, and on radio stations and public forums all over the country. No decisions were drawn, but certain facts became inescapably clear.

So long as the grizzly had not killed, the issue could not have been joined, and the odds against such tragedies remained infinite and immeasurable. But now two had killed and been killed, and by these killings the grizzly had brought about his own demise as a free-roaming denizen of the American West. The end might be postponed by skillful and energetic game management, but it was nonetheless in sight. And Russell wrote, "There is not the slightest room for complacency or blundering, either political or otherwise." But complacency and blundering are commonplace in all human activity, and more so in such outdoor matters as pollution and conservation and the preservation of wildlife, matters to which man turns his attention too late and spends his time eloquently bemoaning his loss.

The grizzly needs space, and the continental United States no longer has space to give him. If he is denied running room, and the human animal continues to bump against him in ever-increasing numbers, the grizzly will maim and kill.

So long as the National Park Service continues to permit more and more humans to flow willy-nilly into all the nooks and crannies of Glacier National Park, no one will need a crystal ball to see the tragedy that is shaping up. A summer or two, perhaps three or four, may pass without serious injury. But inevitably standards will slip, complacency and human error will return, and along will come another grizzly that is peculiar, like the one at Trout Lake, or another grizzly that has been baited into proximity with humans and lost his respect and his fear, like the one at Granite Park. Then more human life will be sacrificed, almost as certainly as tamaracks lose their needles and beavers eat aspen bark. Those who agree with Aldo Leopold will protest, but after the next such rondeau of death in Glacier Park, the grizzly will almost certainly be banished into Canada, and thence perhaps into Alaska to live out his last years as a species, and all the goodwill and understanding in the world, all the good intentions and pious proclamations, will not alter his eventual fate. Man and grizzly are, at core, antagonists, and with the same ingenious tools that fell the giant redwoods of California and strip the topsoil of western Pennsylvania and pollute the streams of Oregon, man will rid himself of his antagonists. The planet is man's; he has bent it to his will and made it his to enjoy, his to develop, and his to destroy. The grizzly will be exiled and then destroyed, and Teasdale's words will be remembered by a few: "What we never have, remains; it is the things we have that go." The grizzly will not return; he will be lost forever, along with the wild frontier on which he lived his final few years as the mightiest animal of the lost American wilderness.